THE EMPEROR'S WARRIORS

Catalogue of the exhibition of the terracotta figures
of warriors and horses of the Qin Dynasty of China.

City of Edinburgh Art Centre
11 September–1 November 1985

**Co-sponsored by Mirror Group Newspapers
and Scottish Daily Record
and Sunday Mail.**

City of Edinburgh Museums and Art Galleries

I.S.B.N. 0 905072 16 2

Published by the City of Edinburgh Museums and Art Galleries, Department of Recreation, City of Edinburgh District Council with the consent of copyright holders Edmund Capon, International Cultural Corporation of Australia Limited, and Jan Wirgin.

Text by Jan Wirgin translated from the Swedish by A.S. Winstanley.

Catalogue entries were compiled in their original form by Lu Shaochen and Lei Congyun.

Contents

City Chambers,
Edinburgh,
EHI IPL

In March 1974, farmers drilling wells in search of water in the Shaanxi Province of China unearthed some large pottery fragments which were to lead to one of the most important archaeological discoveries of modern times: a vast pottery army. Made to guard the burial place of the first emperor of China, the army and the surrounding site is still in the process of being excavated and such is its scale that the excavation will take a team of archaeologists many years to complete.

The tomb of the First Emperor and his accompanying army are situated near Xian, a City with which it was Edinburgh's privilege to be formally linked last April. The close relations established between Edinburgh anbd Xian have now been further strengthened by the People's Republic of China's decision to lend some of the finest objects from the Xian excavation to the City of Edinburgh Art Centre.

The exhibition includes a group of warriors as well as two terracotta horses, and represents one of the great achievements from China's long artistic heritage. It is fitting that Scotland's Capital city should be given this opportunity to display these magnificent treasures from one of the world's greatest civilisations.

Lord Provost

The Qin Empire
with modern provinces

NINGXIA
Autonomous Region

INNER MONGOLIA
Autonomous Region

LIAONING

Great Wall

GANSU

SHAANXI

Beijing
(Peking)

HEBEI

SHANXI

SHANDONG

Yellow

River

Wei River

Lintong

Xian

Xianyang

ANHUI

HENAN

Huai

River

JIANGSU

Yangtze

HUBEI

River

SICHUAN

ZHEJIANG

HUNAN

GUIZHOU
Autonomous Region

JIANGXI

FUJIAN

YUNNAN

TAIWAN

GUANGDONG

ZHUANGXI
Autonomous Region

— boundary of
the Qin Empire

Map of the Qin empire: 221-206 BC.

HAINAN

The Origins of Qin

The state of Qin was founded in the late 9th or early 8th century BC, towards the end of the Western Zhou dynasty, and many centuries before she was to emerge victorious as the ruling house of a unified China. At that time Qin occupied regions of the Wei river valley, remote and geographically isolated from the centre of Bronze Age power and government, in far western lands that are now parts of Gansu and Shaanxi provinces. In this comparative isolation the state of Qin was, for centuries, considered to be something outside the mainstream of Chinese culture.

China enjoyed a degree of political stability and cultural unity under the Western Zhou dynasty (1027-771 BC). The capital of the empire was situated at Hao, close to the modern city of Xian in Shaanxi province, and the territories divided into a number of vassal states whose rulers acknowledged the King of Zhou's suzerainty. However, with the primitive communications available at that time it was inevitable that these feudal states, records note that as many as 150 to 200 such states existed in the 8th century BC, should exercise a certain autonomy. With the passage of time the individual states grew larger, often annexing their less powerful neighbours, and developed their own governmental and administrative structures which further emphasised their independence.

Centralised Zhou control over China was finally eclipsed in 771 BC when 'barbarian' forces (quite possibly armies from the youthful state of Qin were involved) in alliance with rebel Chinese states destroyed the Western Zhou capital at Hao. The royal Zhou line was subsequently established at Loyang, which had been a subsidiary capital during the Western Zhou, in order to bring the seat of government closer to the centre of population and, furthermore, to distance it from the possibility of 'barbarian' attacks from the border regions. The Zhou kings, whilst retaining nominal title under the Eastern Zhou dynasty (771-221 BC), never again exercised any real political or military power. The Eastern Zhou dynasty is traditionally divided into two historical periods: the "Spring and Autumn Annals" period from 770 to 475 BC, and the aptly termed "Warring States" period from 475 to 221 BC.

The former appellation was adopted from the title of a brief chronological record of major events in the eastern state of Lu between 721 and 475 BC. During this time north China, comprising the traditional heartlands of the 'Middle Kingdom', was divided into seven major states: Yen in the northeast (in present-day Liaoning and Hebei provinces and the Beijing (Peking) region), Qi in the east (in present day Shandong province), Lu and Song, both small states to the south of Qi, Jin in the central north (occupying parts of the modern provinces of Shanxi, Shaanxi and Henan), Zhou in the centre (in present day Henan province) and, finally, Qin in her traditional homelands in the far west. South China at this time was dominated by three large states, Qu, Wu and Yue, but these were regarded as 'southern barbarian' states and their affiliations to Zhou supremacy were never strong and when, in the 6th century BC, the rulers of Qu began to call themselves **wang**, 'King'—a term hitherto reserved exclusively for the nominal Zhou ruler, it was clear that this southern state totally rejected any idea of Zhou suzerainty. The other two principal southern states of Wu and Yue soon followed the same procedure.

Throughout the "Spring and Autumn Annals" period the feudal states of North China became increasingly independent, not only from the nominal rule of the Zhou, but indeed increasingly independent of each other. Probably their only unifying feature was their common adherence to traditional Chinese concepts of value, structure in government and society, and responsibility based on the notions of **li** (etiquette) and **yi** (proper relationships).

As the relative independence of the feudal states increased so did their desire to achieve hegemony and thus China gradually descended into the Warring States period, a term fully justified by the incessant warfare between the contending states in their quest for ultimate supremacy. Whilst nowadays the date 475 BC is generally accepted as the starting point of the Warring States period, this is not strictly true. The precipitate event was the dismemberment of the former state of Jin, which began in 453 BC and was finally achieved in 403 BC, into the three states of Han, Wei and Zhao.

These three newly formed states, together with the well established states of Qu, Qi and Yen comprised what were known as the Six States. During the 4th and 3rd centuries BC, these six states fought mercilessly amongst themselves for supremacy. It is significant that the state of Qin, still of her own choice confined in her far western isolation, was excluded from the supposedly all-powerful 'six states'. Thus Qin was able to quietly bide her time and watch the heartlands of China descend into destruction and anarchy. These conditions prompted not only political and social anarchy but intellectual anarchy as well. Dozens of different philosophic schools of thought emerged from the holocaust and thousands of scholars and statesmen travelled from state to state to offer their ideas on a new order. Certainly nobody could dispute the need for a new order and thus the fires of philosophical thought were constantly fuelled and vitalised.

Whilst the principal contending states of north China were in this condition of perpetual conflict and, inevitably, dissipating their resources, the state of Qin was able to develop and strengthen her resources. The gathering strength of Qin was still, nevertheless, largely ignored by the 'six states' for as late as 361 BC Qin was considered to be so outside the realm of China proper that she was excluded from conferences held by the other feudal lords on the grounds that the people of Qin were 'barbarians'.

However, the status of Qin was soon to change radically with the arrival in the middle of the 4th century BC of a notable and powerful statesman, Shang Yang. Lord Shang, as he was to become, was a scion of the ruling house of the state of Wei, one of the 'six states', whose brilliance and vision was neglected by the Wei rulers and who, therefore, deserted his native state to serve the Qin. He is accredited with having introduced into Qin a strict system of rewards and punishments, instituted a new economic and governmental structure, forced the population into productive labour and built a powerful military order that permeated all levels of society and was, indeed, the very foundation of Qin government. In Shang Yang's reforms old and established traditions were set aside for, as he is recorded as saying:

"There are many ways of governing, to benefit the state we need not follow the ancients. Tang and Wu of old ruled as kings without following the ancients, and the Xia and Shang dynasties perished through keeping the conventions unchanged. We must not condemn those who oppose the ancients or praise those who abide by conventions".[1]

Such a disregard for the past would have been considered heresy in Shang Yang's home state of Wei.

The effect of the dogmatic reforms of Shang Yang and the order they imposed are summarised by the Han dynasty historian Sima Qian in his Records of the Historian thus:

"The people were divided into groups of five and then households, mutually responsible for each other. Those who failed to denounce a criminal would be cut in two; those who denounced him would be rewarded as if they had beheaded an enemy; those who harboured a criminal would be punished as if they had surrendered to the enemy. Families with two or more grown sons not living in separate households had to pay double tax. Those who distinguished themselves in war would be rewarded with noble rank according to merit. Those who carried on private feuds would be punished according to their offence. The people had to work hard at the fundamental occupations of farming and weaving, and those who harvested most grain or produced most silk would be exempted from levies. Those who followed subsidiary occupations like trade, or who were idle and poor, would have their wives and sons enslaved. Nobles who failed to distinguish themselves in war would lose their noble status. The social hierarchy was clearly defined and each rank allotted its appropriate land, property, retainers, women slaves and clothing. Those who achieved worthy deeds would be honoured; those who did not, even if they were wealthy, could not make a splendid display".[2]

Although Shang Yang was eventually disgraced and subsequently died in 330 BC his reforms had very considerable impact and coalesced the hitherto relatively dormant state of Qin into a power to be reckoned with. Such were Shang Yang's results that it is recorded in the **History of the Former Han Dynasty** that though

"… the territory of Qin comprised one third of the empire, and the number of its people did not exceed three tenths, yet if we were to estimate its wealth, this would be found to amount to six tenths"[3].

The gathering strength of Qin under the inspiration of Shang Yang's reforms soon became evident to her neighbouring states. Whilst Qin's ever increasing military strength was recognised the state was still considered to be beyond the realm of true China for in 266 BC we find a noble of the state of Wei proclaiming to his king:

"Qin has the same customs as the Rong and the Di ('barbarian' peoples of the north and the west respectively). It has the heart of a tiger or a wolf. It knows nothing about etiquette (**li**), proper relationships (**yi**) and virtuous conduct (**dexing**), and if there be an opportunity for material gain, it will disregard its relatives as if they were animals".[4]

The 4th century BC witnessed the beginnings of Qin's real quest for power in China. At first she adopted the principle of establishing alliances with more distant states, such as Qi in the far east and Yen in the northeast, in order to exert pressure upon her immediate neighbours. With the increasing autonomy of the feudal states such alliances came and went with regularity and little enduring effect, all of which emphasised the political instability of China during the Warring States period. The scale of internecine warfare grew and armies numbering tens of thousands, together with hosts of newly developed cavalry, were thown into battle. Inter-state conferences on disarmament were held frequently but to little avail. A more effective means of establishing alliances was through marriages between the royal houses but in the long term these too succumbed to the onslaught of military power.

The state of Qin's first major territorial advance was not into the heartlands of China, but southwards where, in 318 BC, she defeated and annexed the 'semi-barbarian' minor states of Shu and Ba in the present-day province of Sichuan. In that same year Qin expanded on the horizontal east-west axis and humbled in one enormous and hugely successful campaign the states of Han, Zhao, Wei, Yen and Qi thus giving her, at least, access to control of the whole far north China from her own homelands in the west to the Shandong peninsula in the east. In 312 BC Qin advanced along the vertical north-south axis to defeat the state of Qu, by far the largest of the southern states which had already itself earlier expanded her borders to incorporate the small northern states of Song and Lu, and the southern state of Yue. Following these successes it only remained for Qin to eliminate the already impotent Zhou rulers still located in their central state in the Loyang region. This the Qin achieved in 256 BC, thereby achieving virtual hegemony and bringing in effect an end to the Zhou dynasty.

In many respects it is legitimate to regard 256 BC as the starting date for the unified Qin dynasty. However, in practice this final goal was not achieved until 221 BC when the Qin, under the guidance of Emperor Qin Shihuang, annihilated the last opposing state and thereby proclaimed himself ruler of the new and unified Chinese empire. Qin's rise from a petty state really began with the arrival of Shang Yang in 361 BC and it thus took her a little less than a century and a half to overcome her numerous, if divided, rivals.

Just how a small and isolated state could achieve such an amazing conquest has fascinated the historians of China. All are agreed that Qin's isolated position in the far western periphery was a potent factor. Jia Yi (198-156 BC) in his essay entitled 'Discussions on the Faults of Qin' makes the point:

"The territory of Qin was protected by mountains and girdled by the Yellow River; this is what gave it strength. It was a state that had barriers on four sides...".[5]

The great Legalist philosopher Xun Zi proposed that view in his description of the state after a visit to Qin in 264 BC:

"Its frontier defences are precipitous, its geographical configurations are advantageous, its mountains, forests, streams and valleys are excellent, and its natural resources are abundant. Thus in its geographical configuration it is excellent".[6]

Whilst its geographical location was undoubtedly a military advantage to Qin, it also had other significant consequences. Qin's proximity to the 'barbarian' peoples of the north and the west kept their military machine constantly on the alert and, of course, concentrated her attentions on such military affairs rather than the cultural and philosophical considerations that so dominated the conduct of the central feudal states. The comparative lack of association with and deference to the historical and cultural traditions and values on the part of the people of Qin made it easier for men like Shang Yang to establish new and radical reforms, strict controls and an all pervasive discipline. Xun Zi in his report cited above again commented:

"When I entered its (Qin's) frontiers and observed its customs, I saw that its people are simple and unsophisticated. Their music is not corrupting or licentious, and their clothing is not frivolous. They stand in deep awe of their officials, and are people who follow precedent obediently".[7]

Whilst the Eastern Zhou dynasty, the period which witnessed the gradual and then dramatic emergence of Qin, was one of hopeless division it was also a period of great excitement and enormous change. Stimulated by the division, dissension and warfare that engulfed their country, the statesmen, scholars and philosophers of Eastern Zhou China, led by such eminent figures as Confucius, Mencius and Xun Zi, questioned and analysed their traditional establishments and values. Culturally and philosophically, therefore, it was a period of dynamic growth, energy and creativity that was never to be repeated in the history of China. It was out of this multiplicity of disorder, wide-ranging thought, questioning and, of course, tradition, that Qin emerged as the most powerful and unifying state.

The Great Debate: the flowering of political and philosophical thought

In Chinese civilization philosophy has occupied a place which parallels that of religion in the West. Indeed we may even regard Confucianism more as a religion in China, fulfilling a role like that of Buddhism in the East and Christianity in the West, rather than the philosophy it is. The only religion, as we would regard a formal religion in its concern for other-worldly affairs and the after-life, that gained a foothold in China was Buddhism and that, of course, was an imported tradition. Religion, therefore, played virtually no role in the formation and definition of Chinese society. The emotional, ethical and imaginative concerns that were absorbed in religion on the West were absorbed in philosophy in China.

Philosophy in China was always concerned with practical affairs, of man in society and the organisation and structure of that society. Thus it was the turmoil, conflict and anarchy of the Eastern Zhou period that produced in China what is generally acknowledged to be the 'golden age of Chinese thought'. Amid the destruction of the Spring and Autumn Annals and the Warring States periods, when the established and long accepted social and governmental hierarchies proved inadequate to the purpose of guiding and sustaining the empire, even the most sacred of institutions were being questioned by a growing number of scholars, statesmen and philosophers. These events consolidated the association between philosophy and government, and thus underlined the need for a new philosophical and social ethic to serve as the basis to good government.

The traditions and values that Eastern Zhou China inherited from the earlier Bronze Age dynasties of the Shang (circa 1600-1027 BC) and the Western Zhou (1027-771 BC) were developed out of an essentially patriarchal clan-like society in which there existed a direct line of authority down from the ruler. This fundamental precept gave rise to a strong sense of history and political unity which has subsequently become a feature in the history of China. Religious and philosophical ideas tended to focus on the clan, with ancestor-worship again emphasising the themes of historical identity and continuity. The family-clan pattern in early Chinese society formed the basis for the emergence of authoritarianism in her society and the concept of unity. As this concept was enlarged the structure embodied the city-state society of the Shang dynasty and the centralised authority of the Western Zhou, but the principles of authority relayed through well-defined chains of command from an absolute power, in this case the King, and in yet earlier times the clan or family head, was maintained. Respect for the past and for the great rulers of the past thus became enshrined in ancestor-worship and subsequently into the very heart of the Chinese ethic.

The premise upon which the structure of early Chinese society was built was dependent upon the recognition of certain basic rules of conduct known as **li:** rituals, ceremonies, proper conduct. In the precisely stratified society of early China, with the small minority of 'rulers' and the masses of the 'ruled', such refinements concerned only the 'rulers'. This inevitable abyss in the social structure of early China is described in the **Li Ji** (Record of Rituals) thus:

"The **li** does not extend down to the common people;
punishments do not extend up to the great officers."[8]

The essential function of **li** was to define and make clear the social distinctions in order that everyone's rights and duties were defined and known. In order to maintain these distinctions they were enshrined in a multitude of ceremonial and ritual activities which gave tangible form to the **li**. Thus the proper maintenance of ritual and ceremony was essential to the conduct of good government. The concept of **li**, in its implied sense of identified authorities and responsibilities, also embodied notions of conduct. Confucius in particular emphasised the **li** of antiquity and its associated ritual and etiquette in his belief that inner attitudes and qualities were formed through the practice and refinement of external forms. An awareness of the essential character and pervasive philosophy of the concept of **li** is a prerequisite to our consideration of the principal schools of thought that emerged during the Eastern Zhou period and from which, therefore, the philosophy that led the Qin to victory also evolved.

At the very heart of Chinese philosophy there is, of course, Confucius. The traditional dates for Confucius are 551 to 479 BC and he was, therefore, born at that moment in the history of China when the inadequacies of the old order were all too apparent and the country was on the precipice of descending into the Warring States period. His teachings have been preserved in the **Analects** and take the form of a series of dialogues composed largely of the master's answers to questions.

He was born in the eastern state of Lu but is known to have travelled widely in search of a government post that he considered worthy of his ability and vision. In this respect he was not unlike dozens of other such philosopher-statesmen who wandered the contending states of China at that time seeking an opportunity to put their theories into practice.

Whilst recognising the traditional other-worldly spirits and the existence of an all-providing heaven, Confucius, like his colleagues, expressed little real interest in such matters. To an enquiry about death he replied: "Not yet understanding life, how can I understand death?" Such an agnostic view would have almost certainly been commonplace in late Zhou China.

Confucius felt that the anarchy of his own time could only be redressed by a return to the strict political and social order that had supported the foundation of the Western Zhou dynasty some five centuries earlier. It was essential, in his view, that men should play their role according to their place in a society of strict definition and authority:

"Let the ruler be a ruler, the minister the minister;
let the father be a father and the son a son."[9]

There was no doubt in Confucius' mind that order was necessary and that the distribution of authority according to that order was a preference given by birth. In such views Confucius was a true reactionary but he was more revolutionary in his vision of humanity as a whole for he sought to establish that the qualities of man were not the exclusive preserve of the ruling classes, thereby implying that even the common man had the credentials and qualities of a ruler. Probably Confucius' most substantial contribution to thought and philosophy lay in his belief for the need of strong ethical considerations in government and society. It is this belief that has characterised Confucius as a great and essentially benevolent, if ordered, thinker.

It was, therefore, the virtues of man as an individual and above all, the ruler, that Confucius sought to define and emphasise. Central to this theme were the qualities of **ren** (human-heartedness or benevolence) and **yi** (righteousness). Once when asked about **ren**, Confucius replied: "It is to love all men". Elaborating the point in answer to another such enquiry the master replied:

"Now the man of benevolence (**ren**) wishing to be established himself, seeks also to establish others; wishing to be enlarged himself, he seeks also to enlarge others. To be able to judge of others by what is nigh in ourselves — this may be called the way of benevolence."[10]

Emphasising the role of the family in this conception of an harmonious society Confucius commented:

"Filial piety and fraternal submission!—
are they not the root of all benevolent actions."

The quality of **yi** (righteousness) had its origins in what Confucius considered to be the fundamental 'goodness' of man and thus his inherent awareness of right and wrong. Confucius' great disciple, Mencius, said: "... the feeling of shame and dislike is the beginning of righteousness." With such fundamental and essential qualities man could, through learning and training, acquire **wen** (culture) and **li** (ritual) and thus be morally, intellectually and materially equipped to rule. The outward manifestation of these inherent qualities in the form of **li** was thought by Confucius to be an essential ingredient of good government. The judicious blending of inherent virtue and external ritual reflects the moderation that is characteristic of the Confucian ideal.

Later generations expanded further on Confucian thought and during the later Warring States period two principal, if divergent, schools of Confucian thought developed; one inspired by Mencius (circa 372-289 BC) and the other by Xun Zi (circa 300-237 BC). In many respects these two followers of Confucius represented the extremes of his doctrine. Mencius believed that man was by nature good and that, consequently, man responded to virtue and morality. Education and refinement was of course required in order to realise this fundamental good into worthy and practical virtue. Mencius' most significant contribution, and one which in many ways assisted Confucianism to become the enduring ethic of China, was his belief that man was created morally equal and thus the qualities necessary for government and leadership too were universal among men. Such egalitarianism was a radical notion in late Bronze Age China.

Representing a less idealistic interpretation of Confucius, Xun Zi is generally considered to have founded the 'realistic' school of Confucian thought. Unlike Mencius, Xun Zi believed that man was by nature evil, a condition which could only be remedied by education and culture. Whereas Mencius believed in individual freedom within a society of high morality and virtue, Xun Zi believed that strict control and constant effort were required if culture was to overcome man's inherent evil. His thesis may be paraphrased in a quote from his writings:

"The nature of man is evil; his goodness is acquired by training."[11]
Whilst Mencius and Xun Zi differed widely and fundamentally in their interpretation of the Confucian ethic, both agreed with the need for social and governmental structure, enshrined in **li** (ritual), as the outward manifestation of that inner order. Xun Zi was very much more authoritarian in his approach and indeed it was his philosophy that was to so influence the history of China through his two principal followers, Han Feizi and Li Si, who were responsible together with Shang Yang for the formation of the philosophy of government and society under the Qin dynasty. It was Xun Zi's dogmatic interpretation of Confucianism that became the foundation of the Legalist school of thought which, subsequently, became the adopted philosophy of Qin Shihuang.

Before considering the Legalist school in more depth two further schools of thought should be mentioned in order to cover the spectrum of philosophical thought current in China prior to the Qin dynasty. Mo Zi, who was born around the time of Confucius' death, developed a utilitarian philosophy described in his principal writing, the **Mo Zi**, and known as the Mohist school. Much of his thinking seems to have been inspired by a direct rebuttal of Confucianism on four principles; firstly that Confucius did not believe in God or spirits; secondly that Confucius insisted on elaborate and wasteful funeral ceremonies; thirdly that Confucius emphasised the need for **li** (ritual) in all aspects of society and government which Mo Zi considered both useless and wasteful; and fourthly that Confucius believed in a predetermined fate. Mo Zi sought a kind of utilitarian utopia, in which the Confucian qualities of **ren** (human-heartedness) and **yi** (righteousness) were certainly vital components, but he believed that utopia could only be achieved through universal love and not through the social order and adherence to ritual proposed by the Confucians.

After Confucianism the most important and enduring school of thought in Chinese history has been Taoism. In many respects Taoism represented a general protest against the formally structured code of living philosophy of the Confucians by stressing the independence of the individual. In doing so the Taoists eschewed the rigours of ritual and hierarchy so beloved by the Confucians, just as they eschewed the authoritarianism of Xun Zi and the Legalists. The Taoists maintained that it was the task of man to reach an accord with, and fit into, the great design of nature and not that of man-made society. The great design of nature was known as **dao** (tao), literally the 'way'. Taoists and historians alike have found great difficulty in adequately defining and expressing such an ideal. In essence the **dao** (tao) is that endless and ever-changing self-generating compendium of natural processes and forces that sustains the perpetual evolution of the universe and, thus, nature. For man to conform to and even become part of this whole natural form it was essential that he did not resist it or seek to change it, but to act spontaneously and with purity. Taoism was, therefore, a concept that contrasted totally with the political uniformity and morality of the Confucian school.

Whilst Confucianism and Taoism offered the Chinese people in those troubled times of the Warring States period two broad and differing avenues of thought, there inevitably grew out of these two strains a diverse range of schools of thought that drew something from each. Whilst Legalism grew primarily out of Xun Zi's dogmatic interpretation of Confucianism even that authoritarian school gained something from Taoism, principally the concept of an amoral order in society and a resistance to traditional learning. Similarly the Legalists were influenced by the Mohists in their belief in discipline. However, it was undoubtedly the teachings of Xun Zi that inspired his leading follower, Han Feizi (circa 280-233 BC), in the formation of the Legalist doctrine. It was this doctrine that was adopted by the Qin as the basis for their approach to government and society. Indeed Xun Zi's other great protagonist and colleague of Han Feizi, the statesman Li Si (died 208 BC), was subsequently to become Prime Minister of the state of Qin.

Whilst it must be recognised that all Chinese philosophical schools of thought are concerned to a lesser or greater degree with political science, none was so exclusively concerned with that science than Legalism. The basic premise to Legalist thought was ways and means to consolidate, preserve and strengthen the state. The achievement of this required organisation and commitment and the Legalists adopted Xun Zi's basic thesis of man's capacity in his statement:

> "Man's strength is not equal to that of the ox;
> his running is not equal to that of a horse;
> and yet the ox and the horse are used by him.
> How is this? I say it is because men are able to form social organisations; whereas the others are unable . . . When united, men have greater strength, they become powerful; being powerful they can overcome other creatures."[12]

In order to impose this order on society Han Feizi considered that three traditional factors in politics and government were indispensible: **shi** meaning power or authority; **shu** meaning method or the art of conducting such affairs; and **fa**, meaning law. Fung Yu-lan paraphrases Han Feizi and these factors as follows: "The intelligent ruler is like Heaven because he acts in accordance with law fairly and impartially. This is the function of **fa**. He is like a divine being, because he has the art of handling men, so that men are handled without knowing how they are handled. This is the function of **shu**. And he has the authority or power to enforce his orders. This is the function of **shi**. These three together are 'the implements of emperors and kings'."[13]

Whilst Han Feizi concurred with his mentor, Xun Zi, in believing that human nature was fundamentally evil, he did not accept his teacher's premise that man could be made good, and therefore compatible with the order of society, through education and culture. Han Feizi believed the only method of maintaining the essential order was through a system of rewards and punishments:

> "In ruling the world, one must act in accordance with human nature. In human nature there are the feelings of liking and disliking, and hence rewards and punishments are effective. When rewards and punishments are effective, interdicts and commands can be established, and the way of government is complete."[14]

The Legalists believed in the need for a new order and not one that was based on a return to an ancient order, as that in essence proposed by the Confucianists. In this sense it was a truly revolutionary and radical approach. That Legalism achieved success in its adoption as the governing principle of the Qin dynasty was undoubtedly due to the total collapse of the old order towards the end of the Bronze Age. Under the guidance of Legalist theory all people were forced into productive labour and there was a similar dedication to the development of a strong martial spirit. Merchants, intellectuals and other non-productive and non-martial areas of activity were neither supported nor tolerated. It was therefore an immensely autocratic and dogmatically practical doctrine.

The harsh realism of the Legalists contrasted with the idealism of the Confucianists but such an approach proved to be the only possible solution in unifying a disintegrated empire. In spite of a general condemnation by later generations, Legalism has left an enduring mark on Chinese civilization largely through the eventual, if short-lived triumph, of the Qin. The concept of the centralised state, achieved by the Qin, would not have been realised at that time without the inflexible autocracy of the Legalist approach. However, like so many determined and unforgiving philosophies, it was very much a product of its time and, having achieved a certain goal, it quickly outgrew its usefulness and relevance. Whilst Legalism provided the theoretical machinery for Qin's victory it was also the cause of that state's eventual downfall.

Qin Shihuang: the man and his dynasty

On the evidence of history, both material evidence provided by archaeology and written records, it is apparent that Qin Shihuang was an exceptional man. As a leader he was without equal, although like other relatively uncultured but immensely powerful men, he was temperamental, deeply superstitious and obsessed with a fear of death. Much of the often colourful writing on Qin Shihuang is devoted to his constant search for the elixir of immortality. His extraordinary burial and its impressive guardian army must be seen as reflections of the Emperor's fear of death and yearning for perpetual life.

Qin Shihuang was born in 259 BC, the son of King Zhuang Xiang of Qin by a concubine of the statesman Lu Buwei, whom the king had encountered before ascending the throne and whilst a hostage in the nearby State of Zhao. At his birth Qin Shihuang was given the name Cheng with the surname Zhao. Zhuang Xiang ascended the Qin throne in 249 BC but died just three years later and in 246 BC Qin Shihuang nominally ascended the throne of Qin as King Cheng at the tender age of thirteen. Qin Shihuang's elevation to the throne coincided with the beginnings of his State's serious quest for power. During the early years of his reign when too young to fulfil the duties of office the State was administered by his Prime Minister, Lu Buwei, the man who Qin Shihuang's mother had once served as a concubine.

Lu Buwei was originally a merchant from Yangdi in the State of Zhao who, according to his biography in the **Shi Ji** (Records of the Grand Historian), " . . . by travelling here and there, buying cheap and selling dear, had accumulated a

Qin Shihuang the First Emperor of China and founder of the Qin dynasty.

fortune amounting to thousands in gold."[15] His position in the State of Qin was assured when he provided a favoured concubine to the then crown prince, Zhuang Xiang, and who subsequently gave birth to Qin Shihuang. Having established his position in Qin, become Prime Minister under Zhuang Xiang and the regent in the early years of Qin Shihuang's reign, his power and influence became seemingly impregnable. His biography records that, as regent, he "had some ten thousand male servants in his household." He also, it is recorded, carried on a spasmodic affair with his one time concubine, Qin Shihuang's mother, who by that time had become Queen Dowager. Her conduct was, by all accounts, somewhat reckless and it was another of her affairs that finally led to Lu Buwei's disgrace. He was implicated in a palace scandal, involving the Queen Dowager and a servant who had become intimate with the Queen, that occurred in 238 BC. By that time Qin Shihuang was twenty-one years old and had taken over the reins of government. After the scandal Qin Shihuang, in the following year, dismissed Lu Buwei his former regent who subsequently committed suicide.

The demise of Lu Buwei accelerated the rise in power of Li Si, the great advocate of Legalism who had been a fellow student of Han Feizi under Xun Zi. Although not Prime Minister—Li Si was appointed chief justice—he was arguably the most powerful and influential figure after Qin Shihuang and the king's closest adviser. The combination of Qin Shihuang's authority and determination and Li Si's intellectual and administrative powers led Qin to achieve their final victory and re-unification of the empire in 221 BC.

During the formative years, leading up to the founding of the Qin dynasty, Qin Shihuang—still known as King Cheng of Qin—had become renowned and feared throughout the land as a leader of ruthless determination. As early as 237 BC an adviser to the king of the neighbouring State of Wei had this to say of Qin Shihuang:

"The king of Qin has a waspish nose, eyes like slits, a chicken breast and a voice like a jackal. He is merciless, with the heart of a tiger or wolf. When in difficulties he willingly humbles himself, when successful he swallows men up without scruple . . . should he succeed in conquering the empire, we shall all become his captives."[16]

The numerous histories and records that have documented the life and achievements of Qin Shihuang have all emphasised the strength of his will and determination but, at the same time, dwelt on his weaknesses which seemed to echo the baser instincts of a relatively untutored mind. He did, it seems, need constant reassurance of his power, generally through massive tangible acknowledgements such as palaces, huge armies, untold servants and material wealth.

However, at the very heart of his uncertainty was his constant fear of death and his consequent search for immortality. Having been impressed by certain magical notions, some associated with fringe Taoist thought, Qin Shihuang employed great energies and resources in his search for the elixir of immortality, beginning in earnest in 219 BC. This first serious attempt is described in the **Shi Ji** as follows:

"Xu Shi, who was a native of Qi, together with others, submitted a memorial saying: 'in the middle of the sea there are three supernatural mountains called Peng Lai, Fong Zhang and Ying Zhou. Immortals dwell there. We beg that after we have been purified, we may, together with young boys and girls, go there to seek them.' Whereupon the Emperor sent Xu Shi, together with several thousand young boys and girls, out to sea to search for the Immortals."[17]

These attempts continued but, naturally enough, without success. In 212 BC the Emperor's advisers once again had to report failure in their search and thus recommended that the Emperor should conceal his whereabouts and in so doing pandered to his profound and increasing superstition. One of his advisers, the scholar Lu reported to the Emperor:

"Our search for magic fungus, rare herbs and immortals has come to nothing. It seems some sinister influence was against us. It is my sincere opinion that you would be well advised to change your quarters secretly from time to time, in order to avoid evil spirits; for in their absence some pure ones will come. For subjects to know their sovereign's whereabouts detracts from his divinity. . . . we hope Your Majesty will not let it be known in which palace you are staying, for then we should be able to obtain the herbs of immortality."[18]

The scholar's advice was well received by the ever superstitious emperor as the **Shi Ji** again records:

"'He (the emperor) gave orders for the two hundred and seventy palaces and pavilions within two hundred **li** of Xianyang to be connected by causeways and covered walks and furnished with hangings, bells, drums and beautiful ladies, each in the appointed place. Disclosure of his whereabouts became punishable with death."[19]

Towards the end of his life Qin Shihuang's obsession with immortality and threats to his life and thus his dynasty inevitably distorted his judgment. Two scholars, Han and Lu, amongst the entourage employed to seek the elixir finally abandoned the task as the **Shi Ji** again records:

"No fewer than three hundred astrologers are watching the stars, but these good men, for fear of giving offence, merely flatter the emperor and dare not speak of his faults. It is he who decides all affairs of state, great or small. He even has the documents weighed every morning and night, and will not rest until a certain weight has passed through his hands. How can we find the herbs of immortality for such a tyrant? And so they ran away."[20]

Not surprisingly the Emperor was enraged by such behaviour and disloyalty: " . . . handsomely as I treated Lu and the other scholars, they are libelling me and making out that I lack virtue." Whereupon the emperor ordered the chief counsellor to try the scholars as a result of which, " . . . over four hundred and sixty, found guilty of breaking the law, were buried alive in Xianyang as a warning to the whole empire. Still more were banished to the frontier regions."

Shortly after Qin Shihuang had achieved final victory he embarked upon a series of journeys to far-flung corners of his domain. Stone memorial tablets with inscriptions were created to record the travels. His activities and reactions during the course of these travels, as recorded in the inscriptions, provide yet further insight into the character of the man. His belief that his powers were indisputedly universal are suggested in such incidents as a visit to Mount Tai in 219 BC:

"Then the Emperor ascended Mount Tai. On his way down he was caught in a storm and sheltered under a tree, which was then given the title of Minister of the Fifth Rank."[21]

Even more extraordinary was his violent reaction, later in that same year, when he was thwarted by a great gale in his attempt to visit the temple on Mount Xiang overlooking the Yangtze River. So enraged was Qin Shihuang that he ordered three thousand convicts to cut down all the trees on the mountain, leaving it bare. Some records suggest that he went even further by ordering the entire mountain to be then painted red, the colour of convicts.

Perhaps the most serious reaction of Qin Shihuang to traditional values and learning was, however, his distrust of the great philosophers and scholars of the past. In 213 BC the Emperor held a banquet in his palace at Xianyang for seventy 'learned men'. At this gathering the debate turned to the value and relevance of ancient precedent in matters of government. The Emperor subsequently requested his minister to debate the question. The Prime Minister, Li Si, reported:

> "Now these scholars learn only from the old, not from the new, and use their learning to oppose our rule and confuse the black-headed people . . . Now Your Majesty has conquered the whole world, distinguished between black and white, set unified standards. Yet these opinionated scholars get together to slander the laws and judge each new decree according to their own school of thought, opposing it secretly in their hearts while discussing it openly in the streets. They brag to the sovereign to win fame, put forward strange arguments to gain distinction, and incite the mob to spread rumours. If this is not prohibited, the sovereign's prestige will suffer and factions will be formed among his subjects. Far better put a stop to it!"[22]

The **Shi Ji** then records Li Si's shattering proposal, which the Emperor ratified, and which earned for Qin Shihuang an indelible infamy as instigator of one of the greatest cultural purges in the history of China known as the 'Burning of the Books':

> "I humbly propose that all historical records but those of Qin be burned. If anyone who is not a court scholar dares to keep the ancient songs, historical records or writings of the hundred schools, these should be confiscated and burned by the provincial governor and army commander. Those who in conversation dare to quote the old songs and records should be publicly executed; those who use old precedents to oppose the new order should have their families wiped out; and officers who know of such cases but fail to report them should be punished in the same way.
>
> If thirty days after the issuing of this order the owners of these books have still not had them destroyed, they should have their faces tattooed and be condemned to hard labour at the Great Wall. The only books which need not be destroyed are those dealing with medicine, divinations and agriculture. Those who want to study the law can learn it from the officers."[23]

Thus it was that a huge corpus of the great philosophical writings of early China, and in particular those of the followers of Confucius and Mencius, were destroyed.

In the following year, 212 BC, the Emperor, all powerful yet constantly threatened principally through his failure to find the elixir of immortality, embarked on a massive palace building programme. It was another attempt to bolster his confidence through an outward demonstration of power. The Apang Palace at Xianyang was built with 'terraces that could seat ten thousand'. The **Shi Ji** records:

Drawing of the Qin Imperial palace at Xianyang.

"A labour force of more than seven hundred thousand—men punished by castration or sentenced to penal servitude—was drafted to build Apang Palace and the emperor's tomb on Mount Li. Stone was quarried from the northern hills, timber shipped from Shu and Chu. Three hundred palaces were built within the Pass, and east of it more than four hundred." [24]

Perhaps the most evocative record of all is the description of Qin Shihuang's still to be excavated burial ground in the shadow of Mount Li, to which the remarkable pottery army is the guardian. The construction of the emperor's tomb is recorded in the **Shi Ji** as follows:

"As soon as the First Emperor became King of Qin, excavations and building had been started at Mount Li, while after he won the empire more than seven hundred thousand conscripts from all parts of the empire worked there. They dug through three subterranean streams and poured molten copper for the outer coffin, and the tomb was fitted with models of palaces, pavilions and offices, as well as fine vessels, precious stones and rarities. Artisans were ordered to fix up crossbows so that any thief breaking in would be shot. All the country's streams, the Yellow River and the Yangtze were reproduced in quicksilver and by some mechanical means made to flow into a miniature ocean. The heavenly constellations were shown above and the regions of the earth below. The candles were made of whale oil to ensure their burning for the longest possible death. The Second Emperor decreed, "It is not right to send away those of my father's ladies who had no sons." Accordingly all these were ordered to follow the First Emperor to the grave. After the internment someone pointed out that the artisans who had made the mechanical contrivances might disclose all the treasure that was in the tomb; therefore after the burial and sealing up of the treasures, the middle gate was shut and the outer gate closed to imprison all the artisans and labourers, so that not one came out. Trees and grass were planted over the mausoleum to make it seem like a hill." [25]

Behind this outward display of power and caprice was of course a man of extraordinary vision and achievement. Having defeated the contending states the First Emperor then set about the task of consolidating and unifying his empire. Tough, uncompromising laws and strict adherence to the imposed order of the day were, in his view, the only possible course of action if senses of unity and common purpose were to be instilled into a war-torn and fragmented nation. His first task was to symbolically enshrine his supremacy over the Zhou:

"According to the theory of the Cycle of Five Powers, the emperor decided that as successor to the Zhou dynasty, which was under the Power of Fire, Qin must have the power to vanquish fire. So began the Power of Water." [26]

Aware that unity could only be sustained through law and regulations Qin Shihuang issued a series of edicts within his first year as emperor standardising all aspects of government and society. Another such edict issued in 221 BC states:

"Black became the paramount colour for garments, flags and pennants, and six the paramount number. Tallies and official hats were six inches long, carriages six feet wide, one 'pace' was six feet, and the imperial carriage had six horses. The Yellow River was renamed the River of Power. It was held that to inaugurate the Power of Water there must be firm repression with everything determined by law. Only ruthless, implacable severity could make the Five Powers accord. So the law was harsh and for long there were no amnesties.." [27]

Probably Qin Shihuang's greatest contribution to the practice of government in China was his establishment of the centralised State and the abolition of the feudal system. Again the influence of Li Si was vital for it was he who advised the Emperor against appointing his sons as rulers of the princely states

The burial mound of Qin Shihuang's tomb at Lintong situated approximately 1^1/$_4$ kilometres due west of the buried guardian army.

within the empire on the grounds that, as history had shown, brothers and descendants eventually fall out and "finally set on each other". Li Si therefore advised the Emperor as follows:

"If you give the princes and men who have served you well public revenues and rich rewards, they will be easy to control and there will be no dissension throughout the land. This is the way to secure peace, not by setting up princes."[28]

Thus the feudal system in China was broken and the empire divided into thirty-six provinces, each with a governor, an army commander and an inspector. The edict establishing this constitution continued:

"The common people were renamed the Black Headed People. There were great celebrations. All the weapons were collected and brought to the capital Xianyang, where they were melted down to make bronze bells and twelve bronze statues of giants each weighing two hundred and forty thousand catties, and these were placed in the courts and palaces. All weights and measures were standardised, all carriages had gauges of the same size. The script was also standardised."[29]

Another aspect of the Emperor's deliberate dismantling of feudalism was the legalisation of the ownership of land by all. Whilst peasants had probably been owning land since Shang Yang's reforms in the mid-4th century BC it was only under Qin Shihuang that such ownership became legal. Eventually this freedom of ownership and transfer created a landowning class which led to the exclusion of the peasant farmer.

The **Shi Ji** does not comment further on one of Qin Shihuang's most significant moves in the creation of a unified society: the standardisation of the script. However, the **Qian Han Shu** (History of the Former Han Dynasty) written early in the Christian era, describes in more detail the system of writing in early China and the changes instituted under the Qin.

These comments were further clarified and amplified in one of the most important surviving dictionaries of early China, the **Shuo Wen Jie Zi**, written about 100 AD by Xu Shen:

"When Qin Shihuang first unified the world his Grand Councillor, Li Si, made it uniform according to the standards of the Qin, and did away with those characters which were not in accord with the Qin writing. Li Si made the **Cang Jie Pian**, Zhao Gao, Keeper of the Chariots, made the **Yuan Li Pian** and the **Bo Xue Pian**. They all took from the **large seal** of the Historian Zhou, but in some cases considerably simplified and modified it. This is what is called the **small seal**.

At this time Qin burned and destroyed the classical writings and did away with the ancient records. It made great levies of troops and raised armies, and the duties of the official judges became very complicated. This marked the beginning of the **li** (clerical) style of writing, formed in order to make writing more simple and easy. At this time the ancient script was cut short."[30]

Ensuring the security of his new empire was a major concern of Qin Shihuang. This involved not only the building of ramparts and defensive walls but also constructing and improving a communications system. An imperial road network on an unprecedented scale was built. One such route was opened up in 212 BC as the **Shi Ji** records: "In the thirty fifth year (212 BC) a highway was built through Jiuyuan to Yunyang (the origin of the route was the capital Xianyang, some 800 kilometres from Jiuyuan on the northern border). To make it straight, hills were razed and valleys filled."

Undoubtedly the First Emperor's greatest and most impressive achievement in this respect was his rebuilding and extending of the Great Wall of China. A huge labour force of convicts, 'black–headed people' and disgraced officials was organised to complete the task. Sections of the Great Wall had been built in earlier times during the Zhou dynasty as a means of defence against the marauding nomadic tribes of the northern steppelands. But it was Qin Shihuang who transformed a piecemeal and generally ineffective wall into a continuous line of defence of over 3,000 kilometres in length, stretching from the deserts of Central Asia in the west to the eastern seaboard north-east of Beijing (Peking). The Emperor charged General Meng Tian, who as commander-in-chief of the imperial

A view of the Great Wall of China the construction of which was one of Qin Shihuang's greatest achievements. This photograph shows part of the restored section of the Wall near the Nanjing gate north-west of Beijing.

forces had already distinguished himself in subduing the Xiung-nu Tartars in the far north and north-west, with the task of building the wall. Whilst recorded figures vary, at least 300,000 and probably nearer half a million pairs of hands were employed in the construction of the Great Wall.

The extraordinary outburst of energy that the First Emperor's grand design inspired and the stresses and strains that were caused by such sustained activity and commitment began to show well before the Emperor's death in 210 BC. The **Qian Han Shu** (History of the Former Han Dynasty) comments gloomily, but probably with some accuracy, on the economic situation in Qin China:

> "Having united the empire, Qin Shihuang made public works within, and expelled the Yi and Di tribes without. He received a tax amounting to the greater half (probably this means two thirds), and sent forth as soldiers all to the left of the village gate. The men's exertions in cultivation were insufficient for the grain taxes, and the spinning of the women insufficient for clothing. The resources of the empire were exhausted in supplying the Emperor's government, and yet were insufficient to satisfy his desires. Within the seas there was sadness and dissatisfaction, and this developed into disorder and rebellion." [31]

Qin Shihuang died in 210 BC whilst on one of his travels through the empire. As he died away from the capital, the ever-present prime minister, Li Si, who was accompanying the Emperor, hushed the matter up for fear that there would be trouble among the contending princes at Xianyang. Above all, in such circumstances, Li Si might lose control of the situation. Qin Shihuang had nominated his son Prince Fu Su to succeed and the letter confirming that succession had been entrusted to Zhao Gao, Keeper of the Chariots, for safekeeping and eventual delivery. Like Li Si, Zhao had other ideas on the succession and wished to appoint another son, Hu Hai, whom he had taught writing and could, therefore, more easily influence and control. Thus Zhao and Li Si conspired to destroy the Imperial letter and forge a decree appointing Hu Hai as Crown Prince. Later that same year Hu Hai succeeded to the throne, at the age of twenty-one, and Qin Shihuang was buried at Mount Li.

In spite of his comparative youth and inexperience the Second Emperor immediately sought to emulate his father. Work on the palaces and monuments started by Qin Shihuang was continued, even though the costs in men and materials were more than the empire could bear, for fear of implying that the First Emperor was wrong. In the early years of the Second Emperor's reign the **Shi Ji** records that: ". . . the laws were enforced even more rigorously."

Within months of the Second Emperor's succession the first of a series of revolts against the excesses of Qin rule began to seriously threaten the empire. Local Qin officials, governors, tribunes and magistrates were assaulted and killed with increasing frequency, particularly in the more distant eastern provinces. The prime minister, Li Si, made the reasons for the disturbances quite apparent to the Emperor:

> "The reason for all this brigandage is the bitter burden of garrison duty, building and transport service, and heavy taxation. We propose calling a halt to the work on Apang Palace, reducing transport duties and garrison service." [32]

Under the pressures of a disintegrating empire, cracks began to appear in the hierarchy at the capital. Above all, Zhao Gao saw this as an opportunity to advance his own position and in 208 BC he was appointed prime minister. Almost his first action was to condemn his former co-conspirator and colleague, Li Si, to death. Later that same year the provinces of Yen, Zhao, Ji, Han and Wei all established their own princes as a declaration of independence from the Qin court. Further to the east, rebel armies consolidated and advanced westwards towards Xianyang. The Emperor reprimanded Zhao Gao for not suppressing the rebels and then, concerned at the speed with which the empire was crumbling, the prime minister plotted with his son-in-law, Yen Lo, to overthrow the Second Emperor. In 207 BC Yen Lo confronted and denounced the emperor who, in spite of his pleading even to a request that he be permitted to live as a common citizen, was sentenced to death. Before the troops could be summoned, however, the Second Emperor took his own life. He was succeeded by Zi Ying, son of the Second Emperor's elder brother, as the Third Emperor.

Amid the panic of a rapidly disintegrating empire Zi Ying had his prime minister, Zhao Gao, assassinated. However, his attempts to gain some kind of order were to no avail and in the following year, 206 BC, the Third Emperor submitted to the rebels led by Liu Bang. He it was who established the Han dynasty (206 BC–220 AD), one of the longest and most glorious periods in the history of China.

The Discovery and the Excavation

There could be no more impressive and evocative material expression of Qin Shihuang's vigour and vision than his burial and the newly discovered pottery army. The tomb itself has been described on the evidence of literary records, but it was of course always known from the 40 metre mound that conceals the mausoleum to this day. Whilst this burial mound is the most visible aspect of the Qin Emperor's tomb there are numerous other traces of the mausoleum within the immediate vicinity.

The burial was conceived on the lines of a subterranean palace with, on the surface, a protective outer wall over 2,000 metres in length from north to south and nearly 1,000 metres in width from east to west. Within this extended area was an inner wall that surrounded the burial mound, located in the southern half of the overall compound. The burial pits of the pottery army are situated due east of the northern boundary of this inner wall, approximately $1^1/_4$ kilometres from the burial mound. This location undoubtedly suggests that the function of the army was to guard and protect the entrance to the First Emperor's tomb.

An undertaking of this scale required considerable material resources and manpower and, once again, archaeology has revealed evidence of these within the immediate vicinity. In present day Zheng Zhuan, a village to the north-west of the mausoleum, there have been frequent discoveries of semi-completed stoneworks and iron hammers, as well as iron leg-chains and other such equipment for the holding of prisoners. Approximately $^1/_4$ kilometre to the south-west of the mausoleum has been discovered a 'mass grave', which has revealed a large quantity of human bones, presumably those of labourers who died during the construction work. Other such graves have been found in the same area and, on the evidence of inscriptions on tile fragments from the same sites, it is apparent that these labourers, probably convicts, came from all parts of the empire.

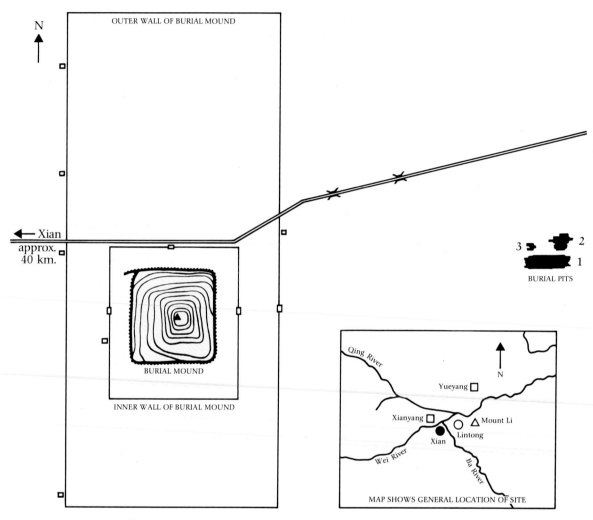

Position of Qin Shihuang's mausoleum to the burial pits of the underground army. At Mt. Li, Lintong. (Distance between Mausoleum & pits approximately 1.25 km).

In the northern half of the mausoleum, within the confines of the outer wall, stone rubble, stone steps and other building materials suggest that this area had been the site for the funerary buildings and sacrificial altars. Since construction of the entire complex would have commenced, as was the custom, when Qin Shihuang ascended the throne and only completed during the reign of the Second Emperor, it is estimated that construction took 38 or 39 years in all.

Some hints that the area around the tumulus might conceal treasures related to the burial were provided by chance finds of isolated pottery figures, five in all, during the years 1932 to 1970. However, these finds gave little indication to the drama of the discovery of the underground army.

It was in March 1974, when local farmers were drilling a series of wells in search of water, that the first finds were made. During this work farmers discovered large pottery fragments, the first tentative finds that subsequently led to the revelation of the First Emperor's buried army. Since that time continual archaeological work on the excavation has revealed three underground pits housing an estimated 7,500 life-size pottery figures of soldiers and horses.

Whilst the three pits vary in size and shape, they are of similar basic construction. Pit number 1, by far the largest, is of rectangular shape, and houses the main body of the guardian army; pit number 2, located approximately 20 metres north of pit 1, is of a more complex shape and houses a smaller guard composed of a variety of personnel and cavalry; pit number 3 located due west of pit number 2, was evidently the command post comprising mainly guards and officers. The overall disposition of the figures determines that the army was facing east, with its back to the tomb, thus confirming its role as one of guardian to the entrance of the Emperor's burial.

The three pits are five to seven metres beneath the present ground level with the figures placed in corridors on an east-west axis. The corridors, divided by earth walls, are paved with pottery bricks on which the figures were placed. A wood construction, with pillars and cross-beams, enclosed the corridors and protected the figures before the topsoil was replaced in order to totally conceal the army. Sloping roadways into the pits were constructed to permit access.

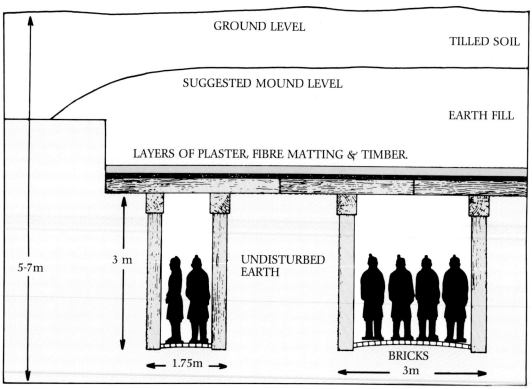

GROUND LEVEL

TILLED SOIL

SUGGESTED MOUND LEVEL

EARTH FILL

LAYERS OF PLASTER, FIBRE MATTING & TIMBER.

5-7m

3 m

UNDISTURBED EARTH

BRICKS

1.75m

3m

Drawing of a cross-section of Pit Number 1 showing the timber framework that was constructed over the corridors housing the pottery figures.

A fallen warrior in the course of excavation.
Opposite: Partially excavated warriors from Pit Number 1.

Pit Number 1

This, the largest pit, is of rectangular form and measures 210 metres from east to west and 62 metres from north to south. The pit houses an estimated 6,000 figures of soldiers and horses.

At the eastern end of the pit is a vanguard contingent comprising 204 soldiers all of which were originally equipped with genuine bows and crossbows. Immediately behind this contingent were placed 30 chariots, each of which was drawn by four horses, and armoured and unarmoured soldiers bearing weapons which included halberds, spears and battle-axes. The remainder of the pit is occupied by the bulk of the army, both armoured and unarmoured soldiers, arranged in nine principal columns of four soldiers abreast, and two columns of single soldiers along the north and south sides. Around the outer edge, on the north and south sides and along the west end, were placed soldiers with crossbows, 518 figures in all, facing outwards as a protective measure to guard the sides and rear of the army.

General view of Pit Number 1.
Opposite: Archaeologists at work in Pit Number 1.

Pit Number 2

Located 20 metres to the north of pit 1 at the eastern end, pit number 2 is not of uniform shape with a roughly rectangular principal area, measuring approximately 84 metres north to south and 60 metres east to west, with a protruding rectangular area at the north-east corner. This extended area measures approximately 27 by 38 metres. This pit was discovered some two years after the discovery of pit number 1, in May 1976. The construction of pit number 2 is in principle similar to that of its larger neighbour, with a timber framework, pottery brick floors and sloping roadways for access. Although very much smaller in number, the figures from this pit are greater in variety and in some respects of greater interest, indicating a more specialised force than the main body of the army.

The protruding north-east area houses four columns of kneeling bowmen, two abreast, totalling 162 figures in all. Surrounding this contingent are 172 standing crossbowmen. All these figures, both the kneeling and standing soldiers, face eastwards. Immediately behind the vanguard contingent are six columns, again ranged in an east-west direction, comprising 25 chariots and horses, chariot drivers, cavalrymen and cavalry horses, armoured soldiers and infantrymen. The cavalry ranks, four horses abreast, are mainly located in the three north-west columns, with a further two groups of four at the rear of the southerly columns of this group.

To the immediate south of this group is a roughly square area occupied by eight columns, also facing east, eight chariots and four chariot horses in each column, making a total of 64 chariots and 256 horses. Each chariot in this group was originally accompanied by a chariot driver flanked by two charioteers carrying long weapons, making a total of 192 soldier figures.

In all it is estimated that pit number 2 contains some 1,400 figures and 89 chariots. The range of figure types, including cavalrymen and horses, chariot horses, kneeling bowmen, charioteers and drivers, and foot soldiers, is reflected in the wide range of weapons found. These include bows, crossbows, battleaxes, halberds, arrowheads, swords and spears. In addition to weaponry, pit number 2 has also revealed a range of other fragments and material, including bronze hinges for the doors that sealed the access to the sloping roadways, bronze linchpins and axle-housings from chariots, fragments of the railings for the chariot sides, evidence of a design in lacquer from the chariots and bronze sections of bits, reins and bridles from the cavalry horses.

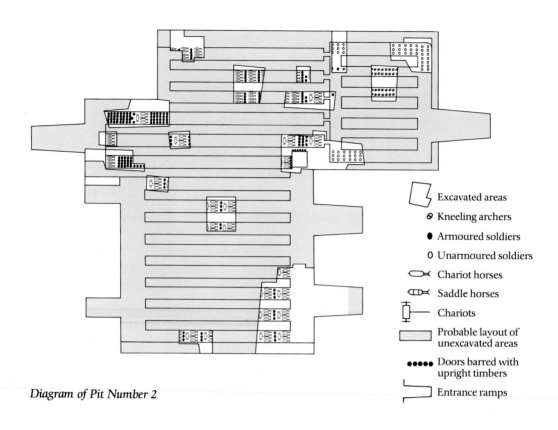

Legend:

- Excavated areas
- ⊘ Kneeling archers
- ● Armoured soldiers
- 0 Unarmoured soldiers
- ⊂⊃⊀ Chariot horses
- ⊂⊡⊃⊀ Saddle horses
- Chariots
- Probable layout of unexcavated areas
- ●●●●● Doors barred with upright timbers
- Entrance ramps

Diagram of Pit Number 2

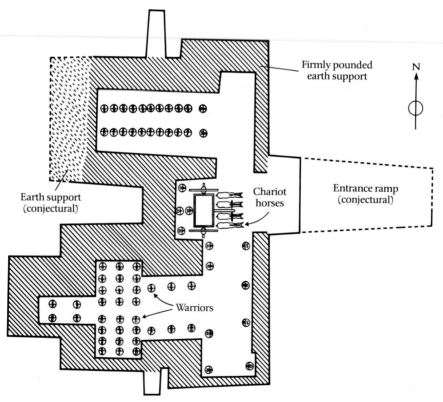

Firmly pounded earth support

N

Earth support (conjectural)

Chariot horses

Entrance ramp (conjectural)

Warriors

Diagram of Pit Number 3

34

Pit Number 3

This is the smallest of the three pits and was discovered shortly after pit number 2. It is located at the north-west corner of pit 1, thus immediately behind or to the west of pit number 2. It is of u-shape, facing west, although the figures within the pit, in accordance with the formation of the entire army, face east. The overall measurements of the pit are approximately 17.6 metres east to west and 21.4 metres north to south. At the front of the pit, that is at the eastern end and confronting the probable location of the entrance, is a canopied chariot followed by four armoured soldiers in full military headgear. In the north and south side chambers, representing the two extensions of the u-form, were positioned small contingents of fully armoured guards numbering 64 in all. The pit was decorated as an army tent and this, together with the ornate canopied chariot and the small, select number of figures, suggests that it was the command centre of the entire army. Furthermore, its position in the far north-west corner of the overall plan ensured that it was well protected by the armies of the two larger pits.

A further pit of rectangular shape has been identified between pits 2 and 3, however, there is no evidence of either structure or figures, which suggests that work on the guardian army of Qin Shihuang was never fully completed. This observation is supported by the apparent absence of a parallel army on the southern axis, for this army, as the plan indicates, is situated at the point that would have been the north-eastern entrance to the spirit road leading to the tomb entrance. Logic and precedent would suggest that a second such army would have been placed to guard the south-eastern entrance. Archaeologists have been following this premise but as yet no material evidence for such a second army has come to light. The building of Qin Shihuang's mausoleum and its accompanying guardian army was of such a scale that it is entirely conceivable that it remained incomplete. As it is, the three pits discovered should, according to archaeologists calculations based on excavations so far, have contained no less than 7,000 life-size pottery figures of soldiers in various guises, over 500 horses and over 130 chariots.

When work on these burial pits was completed and the wood construction covered with soil it has been estimated that the final level of that ground was noticeably above the original ground level. The burial pits were, therefore, like the First Emperor's burial, clearly identifiable. During disturbances at the end of the Qin dynasty, when peasant armies were rising against the stringencies of Qin rule, literary records confirm that the Emperor's burial was attacked. In 207 BC there were two principal rebel forces, one led by Liu Bang who was subsequently to found the succeeding Han dynasty and become its first Emperor under the title of Gao Zu, and the other was led by Xiang Yu who had come from a family distinguished by generations of generals in the previous state of Qu. Whilst the forces of Xiang Yu and Liu Bang were acting in concert against the Qin hierarchy, when final victory was in sight, the two leaders evidently embarked upon independent courses that eventually led to conflict. Although historical records suggest that Liu Bang entered the Qin capital at Xianyang first it was Xiang Yu who killed Zi Ying, the short-lived successor to the Second Emperor, and then ransacked the capital. The **Shi Ji** records these events:

> "A few days later Xiang Yu led his troops west and massacred the inhabitants of Xianyang, the capital city, killing Zi Ying, the king of Qin, who had already surrendered (to Liu Bang), and setting fire to the palaces of Qin; the fire burned for three months before it went out. Then he gathered up all the goods, treasures, and waiting women and started east."

It was almost certainly at this time, 206 BC, that the guardian army burial pits and Qin Shihuang's tomb were also assaulted. This assault is described in the **Shui Jing Zhu** (The Water Classic):

"After Xiang Yu entered the pass, he opened the mausoleum. After thirty days of plundering they still could not exhaust the contents of the mausoleum. Bandits from east of the pass melted the coffins for bronze as well as setting fire to it. The fire burned for more than ninety days."

The tomb has not yet been excavated and thus the accuracy of this report of its plundering cannot be verified, although there seems little cause to doubt it. The burial pits of the guardian army do show signs of having been set on fire by Xiang Yu's rebel army, for charred timbers and pottery fragments and scorched earth are clearly to be seen in the excavated areas, particularly pit number 1. It is almost certain that during this assault the protective timber framework was set on fire causing the construction to collapse and thus causing most of the damage evident today.

Although first discovered early in 1974, work is still continuing on the excavation of pit number 1, now under the cover of a large hangar-like building which serves as an on-site museum. This, together with a small associated museum building displays a range of figures and equipment, was opened to the public on October 1st, 1979. The two smaller pits, numbers 2 and 3, have been partially excavated and are now filled in to await more extensive excavation work at a later date.

The Figures: construction and detail

All the figures, both human figures and horses, were made from a grey pottery. The hardness of the fired body indicates that they may be regarded as earthenware and thus fired at a temperature between 800 and 1,000 degrees centigrade. The appearance of the fired body is not consistent; whilst the majority of the figures are grey, a number are of a slightly reddish hue which suggests that the clay was not necessarily from a single source. This is consistent with the notion that in order to produce such an enormous number of figures several factories and kilns would have been established and the clay used in differing localities may have varied. Whilst the kilns would almost certainly have been in the Xianyang – Xian – Lintong region no convincing evidence for these factories has yet been found.

Investigations into the construction of the figures has shown that the same method was used throughout the entire production. In general the bodies, heads and arms of the human figures are hollow and the legs solid. The legs of the horses are also solid pottery, and these support a hollow body and head. Clearly such large figures could not have been produced from a single mould and it seems they were constructed from a number of separately moulded or modelled segments which were then luted together before firing.

In broad terms the sequence of construction was as follows, for the human figures. Firstly, the feet and legs, of solid clay, were made or moulded and permitted to dry and thereby achieve some solidity. The previously modelled or moulded sections of the torso were then luted on to the base, together with the hollow arms and the solid clay hands. All the joints would have been sealed and strengthened with clay coils. The bases were, it seems, made and fired separately and then added to the completed figure after the firing process.

The heads of the human figures were made in two-piece moulds which were joined together before firing; from the inside a seam is visible between the two ears indicating the joint. This overall moulding would have included certain basic modelling of the features, such as ears, nose, and hair.

However, in order to permit further detail a layer of fine clay was laid over the moulded head to allow detail finishing by hand, probably with a sharp bamboo, of such facial features as the mouth, eyes, moustache and beard, ears and hairstyles. Whilst there is a certain consistency to the faces within each of the varying figure types there are no two identical faces, confirming that each was indeed subject to individual final finish. The heads were, however, fired separately from the figure and are thus, theoretically, interchangeable.

Such hand finishing is also apparent in the detail of the clothing and armour, and again it appears that a layer of fine clay was superimposed over the basic model to permit such detailing. Features such as the armour plates with fixings, belt hooks, shoe ties and costume details could only have achieved such precise representation through hand finishing.

The same principles of construction were employed in the making of the horses. The legs, body, head, ears, mane and tail were all made separately and luted together before the firing process.

The legs of the horses are all solid pottery and the consistency of the shape and form of these legs would suggest moulding with hand finishing. Moulded or modelled sections of the body were then fixed to the legs in sections. The head and neck, separately moulded, were then attached to the body together with detail features such as the ears, forelock, mane and tail, all of which are solid pottery.

Archaeologists restoring a figure of a chariot horse.

Both horse types have round holes in each side of the body, plugged after firing, which permitted the gases and vapours that would have built up in the kiln to escape.

As with the human figures there is an overall consistency in size, shape and style of the two horse types which again suggests that mass production methods were employed. However, there is ample evidence that each model was finished by hand in the varying detail finish of the eyes, nostrils and mouth in particular.

Whilst both the chariot and cavalry horse types are clearly of the same breed, related to the comparatively small but resilient Mongolian pony, there are slight differences in representation which seem to be directed towards emphasising the qualities of the cavalry horse. All the horses, of both types, have four hooves placed firmly on the ground giving them a somewhat static pose. However, the chariot horses lean perceptibly forward as if straining to pull the vehicle while the cavalry horse stands firm and erect.

Both varieties have a square cut mane, a neatly manicured two-pronged forelock and alert ears. The cavalry horse has a long, plaited and pendant tail and the chariot horse a shorter tied tail so as to keep it free of the harness and chariot shaft. The most visible difference between the types is the moulded detail of the

Conservationist restoring the head of a warrior.

saddle and girth on the cavalry horse. Stirrups were not, on the evidence of these figures, in use in China during Qin times.

The range of human figure types represented in Qin Shihuang's army is more extensive; there being seven principle types but with detail variations within each category. The seven broad categories are as follows: officer, kneeling bowman, cavalryman, charioteer, armoured infantryman, unarmoured infantryman and standing crossbowman. The officer class are identified by their greater size and more ornate armour including headgear and small tabs or sashes which may be emblems of rank. The cavalryman is immediately identifiable by the tight fitting helmet tied under the chin, together with tight fitting armour to the waist and flared robe to facilitate riding. The charioteer is identifiable by the fully armoured sleeves and the position of the hands, held firmly out in front as if to hold the reins.

Of the standing soldiers the most dramatic and animated is the standing bowman, with legs set apart in a precipitate pose. The range of armoured and unarmoured soldiers differ in detail features such as hairstyles, facial expressions and the position of the arms which was dependant upon the type of weapon with which the figure was originally equipped. Probably the most attractive and evocative of all the figures is the kneeling bowman, poised on one knee in a firing position.

The attention to detail on all these figures is impressive, particularly in the variety of often ornate hairstyles and headgear. However, similar attention was paid to the detail finish of the footwear and clothing, even to laces and belt hooks. On the kneeling bowman the sole on the visible shoe is shown with the tread pattern. It is this attention to detail which not only assists in the indentification of the varying ranks within the army but also provides information concerning the development of style, fashion and effective armour in early China.

Three basic styles of armour are to be seen in the armoured soldiers from the Qin Shihuang pits. Firstly, a long suit covering the chest, stomach and back, and with separate shoulder plates. This style may be seen on the armoured warrior, catalogue number 9, and the kneeling bowmen, catalogue numbers 2 and 3. The second style is of similar length but the armour plates extend only over the middle and lower sections of the body armour and on the shoulder guards. The third style is for the officer class and includes types with front only armour and front and back armour. In addition the cavalrymen also wear armour, similar to the first style, but slightly shorter and without shoulder plates, in order to facilitate riding. Further variants of these armour styles were used for the charioteers. It is thought that the armour plates used in Qin times, and represented in these pottery figures, were made of iron and linked together with cords, probably leather, and nails, the heads of which are visible on the pottery figures.

Archaeologists have determined that originally the figures were completed with painted detail. Many of the figures so far recovered, including examples in the exhibition, have traces of these pigments. It is thought that a range of twelve to thirteen colours were used, including dark red, rose red, tangerine, pink, purple, dark blue, turquoise blue, green, reddish brown, dark brown and white. Pink was used for faces and hands, with facial details highlighted with black and white. The armour was usually painted brown and the costume beneath red or green. Evidence suggests that the colours most commonly used for the trousers were green or blue. The detail painting would have been applied after the figures had been fired in the kiln.

A number of the figures are inscribed, either stamped or incised, with brief inscriptions of one, two or three characters. The precise significance of these is not yet known although it is thought that they may be the name of the craftsman potter or of the workshop. Yet other figures are inscribed with a single number and again no explanation for these has yet been determined.

Opposite: Conservationists restoring a figure of an armoured soldier.

比例: 1/4   比例: 1/4   比例: 1/4   比例: 1/4

Painted reconstruction of a kneeling bowman.   *Painted reconstruction of an officer.*

比例: 1/4   比例: 1/4   比例: 1/5   比例: 1/4

Painted reconstructions of two armoured soldiers.   *Painted reconstructions of a standing crossbowman and a cavalryman.*

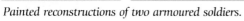

Associated Material

Apart from the pottery figures the three burial pits have revealed the remains of quantities of associated weaponry and related military equipment. It has been noted that each figure was equipped with a genuine weapon where appropriate and the range of weapons is the most diverse and numerous of these supplementary finds. Remnants of buried chariots, pottery rooftile-ends, bronze fittings, fixtures, weights and even bells have been identified amongst the excavated material.

The principal weapons recovered are examples of the dagger-axe, spear-head, halberd, swords, arrowhead and crossbow mechanism. Most of these weapons, with the exception of a small number of iron crossbow bolts, were made of bronze. China had entered her Bronze Age many centuries earlier, in circa 1600 BC, and quickly developed a bronze technology of the highest artistic and technical sophistication. Bronze weapons had, therefore, been in use in China long before the advent of the Qin dynasty. Analysis of selected bronze weapon fragments from the burial pits indicates the metal to be a typical alloy of copper, tin and lead, with much smaller contents of nickel, magnesium and zinc. In addition the swords have a layer, approximately 10 mm in depth, of chromium oxide plating to prevent rust.

Details of excavation in Pit Number 1 showing a bronze crossbow mechanism and a number of bronze crossbow bolts as they were found.

Many of the bronze weapons have a brief inscription, **si gong** meaning 'imperial workshop', testifying that they were indeed the genuine article. Longer inscriptions bearing reign marks and dates have been identified on a small number of bronze dagger-axes and halberds.

Without doubt the most sophisticated of the weapons in use at the time was the crossbow with its most effective bronze firing mechanism. Whilst the performance of the Qin crossbow is not documented, similar weapons were in use during the succeeding Han dynasty and literary records state that such weapons could fire a bolt a distance over 200 metres. The bow itself was made of red lacquered wood.

Among the non-weaponry bronze items that have been recovered the most numerous are various fittings and fixtures, such as linchpins, crossbar ornaments and decorative features, from the chariots. A number of bronze hinges for the access doors and horse's bits, harness and rein fittings have also been recovered. A smaller number of iron fittings and equipment of a more utilitarian nature, such as hammers, hoes, nails, spades and shovels have also been found.

Although the chariots, of wood construction, have long since perished through the collapse of the pit and long burial, archaeologists have been able to accurately assess their size and design from fragments and the evidence of the impressions in the surrounding earth. All the chariots had a single shaft, to which was attached a crossbar linking the four horses. The shaft, approximately 3.7 metres in length, was connected to the underneath of the vehicle box. The measurements of the chariot box appear to have varied although an average size might be estimated at 150 cm in width and 120 cm in depth—sufficient space for a single charioteer and no further personnel. The average diameter of the multi-spoked wheels may be estimated at 180 cm. The comparatively ornate balustrades on the sides and front of the box were constructed of wood and decorated with a characteristic geometric diaper pattern in lacquer.

The Bronze Chariots

The area around the First Emperor's grave will continue to offer many new surprises, and this is shown by the find of two bronze chariots, excavated in December 1980. These are, in their own way, even more remarkable than the terracotta army.

The chariots, each harnessed with four horses, were found about 20 metres west of the burial ground at a depth of 7–8 metres between the inner and outer wall of the burial ground. It is supposed that they constituted part of an imperial burial procession. One of the two chariots has now been restored and can be viewed in its full glory in a separate museum.

Both chariots are of the same type, with an axle and two wheels, harnessed with four horses and a charioteer all made of bronze. The larger chariot, which is shown in the illustration, was made in half scale and is 2.86 metres long, 1.07 metres high and weighs 1,241 kg.

The chariot was made entirely of bronze, as opposed to the wooden chariots found in the pit, and as all the pieces were preserved one can now observe in detail how a chariot from this era was made. The chariot is of a very special construction and is probably a copy of one of the special chariots used by the court. One of the reins carries the inscription "AN CHE" which can be interpreted as "comfortable" or "luxury carriage", and indicates that this was the type of carriage primarily used by the empress, princesses and the imperial concubines. Carriages of this kind were also used by the emperor himself for longer journeys around the country and it was probably in a chariot like this that he made his last journey in secret back to the capital, concealed in his coffin.

The chariot is completely covered, the roof consists of a parasol-like canopy that spreads over the sides and also protects the open front part where the charioteer is kneeling. The entrance to the chariot is at the back and on the other three sides are windows for ventilation. The sliding shutters are slatted and through them the traveller—sitting or lying down—could see out without being seen.

The horses and the chariot are elaborately painted. The basic colour is white, with red, green, blue, purple and black decoration. The inside of the chariot is also decorated with paint and fragments of silk show that it was originally silk-lined. The details are very delicately worked and the harnessing is decorated mainly in gold and silver. The kneeling charioteer is very detailed, there is a sword by his side and he wears an elaborate headdress which is tied under his chin.

The execution of the carrriage is an example of extraordinarily advanced technology. A series of very complicated methods of casting, jointing and construction were used. The size of the canopy-shaped roof is more than one metre square, but it is only 2–4 millimetres thick, the casting perfect and even. The underside consists of 36 bow shaped struts, each 6 millimetres thick. The equipage, worked with the greatest precision, is made up from 3,462 parts, in gold, silver and bronze.

Artistically, the bronze chariots are even more convincing than the terracotta figures and show that the artists of the Qin created a new and powerfully realistic style of sculpture of which we were previously not aware. As has happened so often, the historical sources of the Chinese have been proved to be true. When one sees the mighty bronze horses and their chariot, one is reminded of the description in the **Shi Ji** of what happened after the First Emperor united the country, when all the weapons in the empire were collected and taken to the capital Xianyang where they were melted down and bronze bells and twelve giant bronze figures were cast, and put up in the palaces.

The find of the bronze chariots shows that the bronze craftsmen of the Qin Dynasty could very well have manufactured bronze figures of this size.

One of the bronze chariots after restoration.

Epilogue

During the earlier part of the Chinese bronze age, in the Shang and the Western Zhou, art was almost exclusively a religious concern. The massive, bronze sacrificial vessels used in the princely, ancestral temples and for offerings to the various gods of nature, dominated artistic production. All small objects produced from jade, bone, marble and other materials were decorated with religious symbols. This situation changed during the last stage of the bronze age, the period we usually refer to as the Spring and Autumn Annals and the Warring States. A completely new cultural climate was created as a result of far reaching political and social upheaval and the strong economic upswing that marks this warring period.

Religion was no longer the driving force behind the arts, increased affluence bringing with it the growing importance of the profane arts and a demand for objects of art by a greatly enlarged spectrum of the population. There was a break with old traditions, and greater artistic freedom was enjoyed.

The political division into small independent states created many regional art centres, with more or less distinctive styles, and a diverse artistic production developed. Bronze still dominated the decorative arts but other materials such as jade, glass, gold, silver, lacquer, wood, pottery and silk grew in importance. It could be said that the foundation for subsequent Chinese decorative art is laid during this era. For the first time the Chinese brush is used in script and for painting, and the first painted silk appears. Sculpture also made great progress; this can be seen particularly in small, round, bronze sculptures of realistic animals and in some cases, human beings. Sculptures in lacquered wood and pottery also occur. Usually these sculptures were produced on a relatively small scale.

Until now, very little has been known about the art produced during the short reign of Qin. Historians have readily treated the Qin Dynasty as "semi-barbaric", and did not expect them to be capable of more advanced artistic production. However, historical sources described how the First Emperor filled his newly erected palaces and his mausoleum with treasures, although no finds that could be connected with the independent artistic activity in the Qin Empire had been previously discovered. The only discoveries were a few decorated roof tiles and burial tiles from the area around the former capital Xianyang, and the emperor's burial mound.

The only indication that something of real interest might be found near the grave was the occasional discovery of large terracotta figures such as kneeling servants found between 1932 and 1970. The discovery of a whole army of life-sized terracotta sculptures was therefore a sensation and utterly unexpected when it occurred in March 1974.

During the early bronze age people and animals were offered in connection with the burial of kings and princes and they, together with weapons, household utensils and ornaments followed the dead into the grave to serve him in his afterlife. The human offerings ceased to a great extent during the latter part of the bronze age. Wooden and straw dolls were then introduced as followers, and later these were also made of stone and terracotta. The tradition of putting terracotta figures in the grave was until now considered to have been developed primarily during the Han Dynasty, and the majority of the figures that occurred then are fashioned in a relatively small format, quite different from the monumental scale of the Qin soldiers.

From an art historical viewpoint this mighty, realistically made terracotta army stands completely isolated. It has no predecessors and, as far as we know, it has no immediate followers.

The Qin figures are also a sensational step forward technically. Not only skilled craftsmen but also a deep knowledge of ceramic technology and access to kilns of a size one did not think existed at this time were called for to be able to manufacture and fire sculptures of this size. To create this large monument to himself Qin Shihuang must have not only summoned the greatest sculptors in the country, but also gathered a host of qualified craftsmen and skilled potters and constructed large workshops in the vicinity of the capital.

The figures are also artistically remarkable. The realistically fashioned faces that give the viewer a feeling of an individual portrait are executed with a liveliness and sculptural sensitivity that is quite unique. They differ considerably from the stereotyped faces which usually meet us in the terracotta figurines from later burial art. It is above all this personal radiance which makes the Qin army figures so gripping. On closer examination one finds however that the treatment of the body is not as advanced as that of the faces. The anatomy is incorrect and the majority of the soldiers are rendered in static poses, facing frontally and standing stiffly. The slightly varied positioning of the arms is the only distinguishing feature. Only a few figures, the standing and kneeling crossbowmen, express more liveliness and a sense of movement.

It is primarily through the individual facial expressions and the many personal and delicately executed details in the robes and armour, that the soldiers stand out as separate personalities.

Finally it is the size and overwhelming number of these sculptures that make such a strong and lasting impression on the observer. It was surely this vision of grandeur, overpowering numbers and irresistible power that the emperor sought to create with this mighty army. It is a fitting monument to Qin Shihuang's remarkable personality, his dreams of greatness and longing for immortality.

Opposite: General view of Pit Number 1.

Notes

1. Yang, Hsien-yi and Gladys; **Records of the Historian (Shi Ji)** by Sima Qian, Peking 1979, p.63.
2. Yang; **op. cit.,** p.63.
3. **Qian Han Shu** (History of the Former Han Dynasty), ch. 28b.
4. Bodde, D; **China's First Unifer,** Leiden 1938, p.3.
5. Bodde, **op. cit.,** p.6.
6. Bodde; **op. cit.,** p.9.
7. Bodde; **op. cit.,** p.9.
8. **Li Ji** (Record of Rituals), ch. 10. Quoted Fung Yu-lan; **A Short History of Chinese Philosophy,** New York 1948, p.155.
9. **Analects XIII.** Quoted Fung Yu-lan, **op. cit.,** p.41.
10. **Analects XII.** Quoted **Hsiao Kung-chuan; A History of Chinese Political Thought,** Princeton University Press 1979, p.102.
11. **Xun Zi,** ch. 23. Quoted Fung Yu-lan; **op. cit.,** p.145.
12. **Xun Zi,** ch. 10. Quoted Fung Yu-lan; **op. cit.,** p.146.
13. Fung Yu-lan; **op. cit.,** p.158.
14. Fung Yu-lan; **op. cit.,** p.162. For a fuller translation see Burton Watson; **Han Fei Tzu; Basic Writings,** Columbia University Press, New York 1964, the chapter 'The Way of the Ruler'.
15. Burton Watson; **op. cit.,** p.36. Chapter 85 of the **Shi Ji** and devoted to a biography of Lu Buwei.
16. Yang; **op. cit.,** p.162. From another chapter in the **Shi Ji** devoted to a biography of Qin Shihuang.
17. Bodde; **op. cit.,** p.115.
18. Yang; **op. cit.,** p.179.
19. Yang; **op. cit.,** p.180.
20. Yang; **op. cit.,** p.181.
21. Yang; **op. cit.,** p.169.
22. Yang; **op. cit.,** pp.177-8.
23. Yang; **op. cit.,** p.178. The 'Burning of the Books' is discussed at greater length in Bodde; **op. cit.,** pp. 80-4.
24. Yang; **op. cit.,** p.179.
25. Yang; **op. cit.,** p.186.
26. Yang; **op. cit.,** p.167.
27. Yang; **op. cit.,** p.167.
28. Yang; **op. cit.,** pp.167-8.
29. Yang; **op. cit.,** p.168.
30. Bodde; **op. cit.,** p.148.
31. Bodde; **op. cit.,** p.172.
32. Yang; **op. cit.,** p.191.

CATALOGUE

Exterior view of the main museum building at the Qin Shihuang burial pits' site, Lintong. The large structure houses the excavated Pit Number 1 and was opened to the public on the 1st October 1979.

1
Standing Crossbowman
Height: 178 cm
Excavated in 1977 from Pit Number 2
Shaanxi Museum of Qin Dynasty
Terracotta Warriors and Horses, Lintong.

    The figure stands in a positive almost defiant manner, the feet set apart with the right foot turned outwards and the left foot forward. Unlike the other standing figures from the burial pits the standing crossbowman does not adopt the strict frontal pose and displays a degree of naturalism in the animated stance. The pendant left arm and tightly held right arm are clearly poised as if to hold a crossbow. The impression of alertness is completed by the careful tilt of the head.

    The crossbowman is dressed in an unarmoured battle robe, fastened around the waist with a belt and belt hook, short boots and leg protectors. The hair is tightly coiled into a neat bun on the right side of the head.

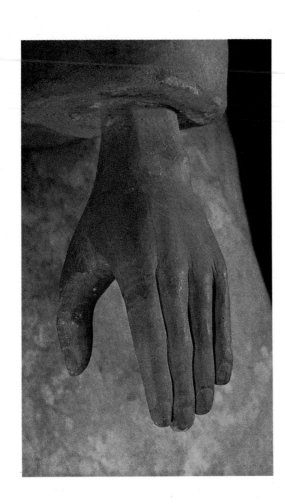

2
Kneeling Crossbowman
Height: 122 cm
Excavated in 1977 from Pit Number 2
Shaanxi Provincial Museum, Xian.

The figures of kneeling crossbowmen, all of which were recovered from pit number 2, are basically similar but with slight detail variations. This example adopts the characteristic pose, resting on the right knee with the left knee raised. The right arm is held towards the right thigh with the hand open and ready to hold the weapon. The left arm rests on the raised left knee and the hand extended across the chest in order to hold the crossbow. Particularly characteristic of the figure type is the straight, almost arched back which emphasises the impressions of concentration and discipline. The head is held firm and the eyes look directly ahead.

The crossbowman wears plated armour on the upper half of the body together with shoulder pieces. The battle robe beneath is distinguished by the series of pleats and folds as it rests over the legs. The square cut shoes feature the tread of the sole in great detail.

The hair is tied in a decorative plait on the back of the head and then coiled into a bun tied with ribbons. On the head, face and hair, traces of the original pigments may be seen.

3
Kneeling Crossbowman
Height: 122 cm
Excavated in 1977 from Pit Number 2
Shaanxi Museum of Qin Dynasty
Terracotta Warriors and Horses, Lintong.

    This figure of a kneeling crossbowman is fundamentally similar to catalogue number 2, with some detail distinguishing features. The right arm on this example is held slightly higher, with the elbow held back and, as if to heighten the sense of alertness, the head too appears to be raised with a longer neck. Slight differences to the facial features, in particular the moustache, may also be noted. The hair, whilst ornately plaited in the style of the previous figure, is tied into a bun on the right side of the head. Another distinguishing feature is the absence of pleats on the battle robe.

4
Cavalryman
Height: 180 cm
Excavated in 1977 from Pit Number 2
Shaanxi Provincial Museum, Xian

All the figures of cavalrymen so far recovered were placed in Pit Number 2, together with cavalry horses. The figures are generally consistent in pose and overall detail. This example has the short tight-fitting armour on the upper half of the figure and, in common with other cavalrymen, no shoulder plates and no sleeve armour. Beneath the belted waist the robe appears full with pleats and folds. The stitched leather shoes are represented in some detail with lacing and ties.

Similarly characteristic of the figure type is the small tight fitting cap fastened under the chin. According to excavation reports it is thought, on the evidence of paint remains, that such caps were originally painted a reddish brown, suggesting leather, with an all-over decorative pattern of red dots in groups of three. The hair is plaited into a chequered pattern on the back of the head. The face is distinguished by the firm and determined features and the flowing moustache. Originally, he held a bow in his left hand and the horse's reins in his right.

5
Cavalry Horse
Height: 172 cm; Length: 203 cm
Excavated in 1977 from Pit Number 2
Shaanxi Provincial Museum, Xian.

The horse stands erect and immobile with four hooves firmly planted on the ground. The head is raised and the ears pricked thus lending the figure a sense of preparedness. The moulded saddle with hand-finished carved and incised detail probably represents a leather original. On the surface of the saddle are modelled a series of black circles representing tacks, which were painted red, white, brown and blue. Around the pommel of the saddle are tassels and ribbons. The saddle is held in place by a girth underneath the belly of the horse. The shape and style of the saddle is similar to modern versions with the exception that stirrups were not, it seems, known in China at that time.

When this horse was unearthed the bit of its bridle was still in place in the mouth. Around the horse were bronze bits, bronze rings and ornamental harness fittings. After restoration work the protective head cage and reins were reconstructed. There are two reins, each approximately 1 metre in length; one end of each was joined to the bit with two large rings and to the other end was attached a scissor-shaped bronze ring to enable the rider to hold the reins. The reins themselves were made of a bronze chain or string and small square limestone pieces.

6
Uniformed Warrior

Height: 196 cm
Excavated in 1979 from Pit Number 1
Shaanxi Museum of Qin Dynasty
Terracotta Warriors and Horses, Lintong

This soldier is not wearing armour. The right hand held a long weapon and the left hand is pendant. He is dressed in a light battle robe, and the belt around his waist is fastened with a distinctive belt-hook. He wears short trousers underneath the robe and laced boots on his feet. The expression on his face is firm and determined, qualities which are emphasised by a full moustache. A small cap with a chin strap sits on his head and the hair on the back of his head is plaited into a chequered pattern.

7
Charioteer

Height: 190 cm
Excavated in 1977 from Pit Number 2
Shaanxi Museum of Qin Dynasty
Terracotta Warriors and Horses, Lintong

    This figure is a chariot driver. He wears a battle robe and armour and has both hands stretched out in front of him as if holding the reins in a tight grip. The ornate headgear and the plaited hair gives the figure an air of dignity. The charioteer was found beside the fifth chariot in the first column in the southern part of Pit number 2. This area is occupied by 8 columns of chariots with 8 chariots in each; a total of 64 chariots. Each chariot was manned by a chariot driver flanked by two soldiers in armour carrying long weapons. Various types of armour were used depending on which battalion the crew belonged to. This figure wears a cuirass without shoulder plates or sleeve armour, the most common form of dress for charioteers in Pits 1, 2, and 3. The type of armour where the shoulders as well as arms down to the wrists were protected by plates is only found in Pit number 2 and is a type of armour which originates from the Warring States period and is not used after the Han Dynasty.

8
Warrior

Height: 183 cm
Excavated in 1974 from Pit Number 1
Shaanxi Museum of Qin Dynasty
Terracotta Warriors and Horses, Lintong

The figure is erect and is dressed in armour with shoulder plates. The chest and backplates are firmly riveted together whilst the other parts are jointed to give freedom of movement in combat. The right arm is raised as if he held a long weapon. With the exception of crossbowmen, the majority of footsoldiers at this time carried spears and that was probably the case with this soldier. It is known that during the Western Han Dynasty the infantry was issued with shields carried in one hand. There is no proof, however, that this was the case in the Qin Dynasty. Spearheads of bronze, about 15.3-17.5 cm long, fitted to wooden staffs, have been found. An 11 cm long bronze casing was fitted to the other end of the staff.

9
Officer in Armour

Height: 184.5 cm
Excavated in 1974 from Pit Number 1
Shaanxi Museum of Qin Dynasty
Terracotta Warriors and Horses, Lintong

This figure, representing an officer, is dressed in battle robe with short trousers and wears armour with shoulder plates of a similar type to figure number 8. The legs are protected by leg shields under which the broad angular boots protrude. It can be seen by the position of the hands and arms that the figure held a long weapon in the right hand. His headdress is ornate and on the back of the head his hair is plaited into a chequered pattern. Similar to other officers the figure has a confident and dignified expression.

10
Kneeling Stableboy

Height: 68 cm
Excavated in 1976 from the Horse Pit at
Shangjiao Village east of Qin Shihuang's
grave.
Shaanxi Museum of Qin Dynasty
Terracotta Warriors and Horses, Lintong.

This figure was excavated together with 19 similar terracotta objects.

Close to the village Shangjiao, approximately 350 metres east of the outer wall that surrounds the burial mount of Qin Shihuang, there are two pits in a north-south direction. Parts of the pits contain terracotta warriors and horses. Another part consists of holes where horses were buried alive. Over a stretch of approximately 1500 metres north to south there are 93 such holes of which some have been excavated. The horses were buried one at a time, in one pit, together with terracotta stableboys, tools and fodder.

The figures are dressed in full length robes and kneel upright. The hair is plaited and tied up at the back. They all have individual facial expressions and the position of the hands also varies from figure to figure.

Originally these figures were painted but only traces of pigment remain. The hair was black, the face and hands skin coloured, and the robe was painted green or red with the sleeve turnups green or purple.

The head, hands and body were made separately and assembled prior to firing.

11
Chariot Horse

Height: 171 cm
Length: 226 cm
Excavated in 1974 from Pit Number 2
Shaanxi Museum of Qin Dynasty
Terracotta Warriors and Horses, Lintong

The tied tail of the chariot horse and the lack of saddle are two of the more obvious distinguishing differences between it and the cavalry horse although they are of similar look and breed. The chariot horse also has a slight forward leaning pose which indicates the strain of pulling a chariot. It is somewhat longer with shorter legs than the cavalry horse. This breed of horse has survived in the Sichuan province in Western China and is today used as a carthorse. This particular exhibit was excavated from the southern corridor of Pit number 2, and it is estimated that there are 256 such horses in that part of the pit.

12
Bronze Sword

Total length: 91.5 cm
Length of handle: 19 cm
Excavated in May 1981 from Pit Number 1
Shaanxi Museum of Qin Dynasty
Terracotta Warriors and Horses, Lintong.

The sword was discovered intact from trench 1 in pit number 1 and is in a re-markable state of preservation. Originally, the sword would have been kept in a wooden scabbard which has perished with the exception of a bronze surmount.

The sword blade is narrow and thin with a ridge along the centre. According to analysis the principal metals used were copper and tin, with a higher percentage of tin (21.3%) than in other bronze pieces from the excavation. This higher tin content resulted in an increased hardness comparable with tempered carbon steel. The surface of the sword contains 0.6 to 2.0% chromium, with a thickness of .10 to .15 mm, which acted as a protective coating against corrosion during the long burial.

In style and appearance the sword resembles the classic Zhou sword which continued to be used in the succeeding Han dynasty. Iron swords of similar shape, dating from the later Zhou, Qin and Han dynasties have also been found at other sites. Many bronze swords of this type have additional ornament, generally in the form of turquoise, gold, silver or jade inlay at the guard and in the top surface of the pommel. The plain solid hilt in this example would originally have had a binding to ensure a safe grip.

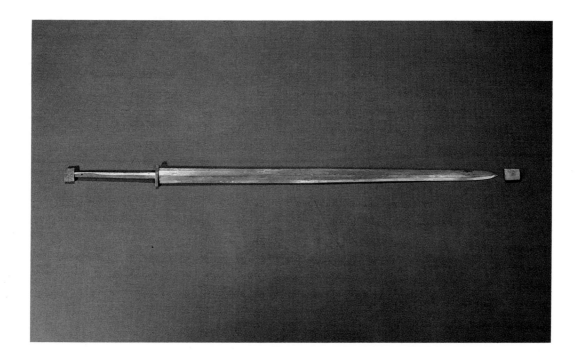

13
Bronze Crossbow Mechanism
Length: 8 cm
Height: 16.2 cm
Width: 3.6 cm
Excavated in 1979 from Pit Number 1
Shaanxi Museum for Qin Dynasty
Terracotta Warriors and Horses, Lintong.

This trigger mechanism for a crossbow is a type that, having been invented towards the end of the Zhou Dynasty, quickly found favour and was widely used to great effect. The mechanism was made in four separately cast pieces and precision in the manufacture was essential for efficient working.

The bronze crossbow mechanism was very much more powerful than any of its contemporary weapons as it could, reputedly, fire a bronze bolt a distance of 200 metres (650 feet). Its importance in ensuring military supremacy over China's marauding "barbarians" on her northern and north-western borders was considerable. The mechanism was of equal significance and in widespread use during the succeeding Han Dynasty. A number of excavated Han examples have brief inscriptions, often incorporating a date. This Qin example is inscribed with a single character, "**geng**", (the 7th of the ten Heavenly stems) in two places and is probably a serial number.

14
Bronze Crossbow Bolts
(20 examples)
Length: 17.2 to 20 cm
Excavated in 1976 from Pit Number 1
Shaanxi Museum of Qin Dynasty
Terracotta Warriors and Horses, Lintong.

The pointed heads of the bolts are triangular cones with equal sides which were cast independently of the circular stems. Analysis has shown the composition of the bronze to be similar to that of the crossbow mechanism (catalogue number 13), an alloy of copper and tin with small lead and zinc contents. The surface contains a layer of chromium oxide to provide an extra hardness and durability, like the sword (catalogue number 12).

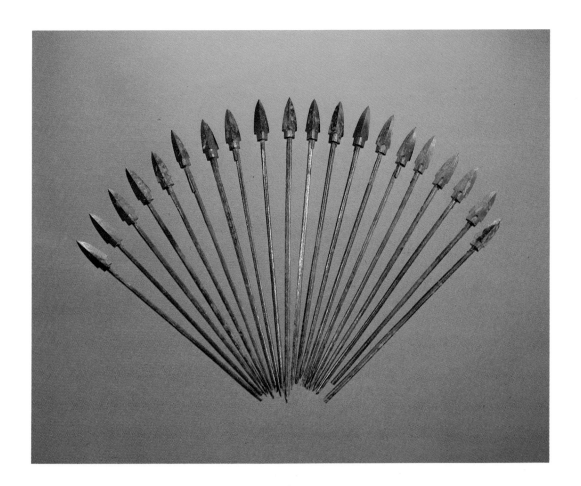

15
Reconstruction of a Crossbow
Length: 140 cm
Shaanxi Museum of Qin Dynasty
Terracotta Warriors and Horses, Lintong.

This reconstruction of a Qin Crossbow was made on the evidence of fragmentary remains and impressions in the surrounding earth of an example buried in Pit Number 1, where a large number of the pottery soldiers were equipped with these weapons. The original crossbow would have been made of wood and painted, or possibly lacquered, red. The body of the bow is 71.6 cm in length, with a groove at the front in which the bolt rested and the bronze trigger mechanism at the rear.

Whilst the composite bow had been known in China since Shang times the mechanically triggered bow, such as this example, appeared only in the late Zhou period. These earliest examples, dating to around the 4th century B.C., had a simple firing mechanism without the casing seen on Qin examples, such as catalogue number 13, and on this reconstruction.

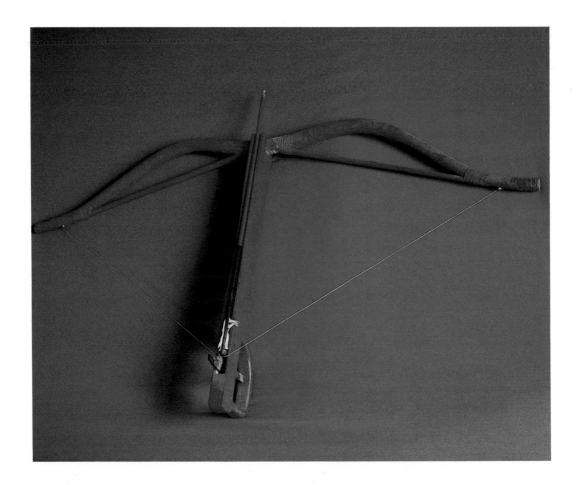

16
Model of a Chariot (¼ scale)

Length: 121 cm
Width: 82.5 cm
Height: 46 cm

Shaanxi Museum of Qin Dynasty
Terracotta Warriors and Horses, Lintong.

This reconstruction of a chariot was made on the basis of fragmentary evidence and impressions from an example that was buried in pit number 1. All chariots of Qin date were made of wood and those that were buried have, therefore, largely perished not only through natural decay but also through the fires that occurred during the rebel assault on the pits at the end of the dynasty.

The chariot is rectangular in shape with openwork wood railings along the front and sides. A raised horizontal bar, for the charioteer to hold, is fixed towards the front of the vehicle. The wood was evidently painted with classic geometric designs in lacquer. The single shaft is attached to the underneath of the vehicle with a crossbar for the harnesses of the four drawing horses.

The chariot was known in China as early as the Shang dynasty as fragments have been discovered in a number of mid to late Shang royal tombs of circa 1300 BC. Many ornate and sophisticated bronze fittings, such as linch-pins and axle-caps, of Shang and Zhou date chariots have been recovered from tombs and burials. The chariot thus became a significant factor in military affairs in Bronze Age China and historical records make numerous references to battles involving large forces of chariots and troops. One such reference describes a battle, in 589 BC, between the states of Jin and Qi in which 800 chariots and 12,000 men took part. Whilst undoubtedly refined in some respects, this Qin example is the natural successor to those chariots of Bronze Age China and the forerunner to those of the Han dynasty. During the Han and subsequent dynasties the chariot continued to be used but was gradually superceded by the quicker and more effective cavalry.

17
"Half Tael" Copper Coin
Diameter: 3.4 cm
Thickness: 0.2 cm
Weight: 11 grams
Excavated in Guodu village,
Changan county, Shaanxi Province.

Round coinage with a square hole for stringing a cord, such as this example, was introduced by the Qin as one of the many standardisation measures. Prior to the introduction of such coins the principal forms of currency in China had been 'knife' and 'fabric' money which were much less conveniently circulated than these small round coins, which continued to be the basic model for coinage in China until the end of the Qin dynasty in 1911.

The two characters cast in relief either side of the square hole indicate the value of the coin and read **ban liang**: 'half tael', a tael being a unit of weight for silver.

18
Tiger-Shaped "Yangling" Bronze Tally Inlaid with Gold (Reproduction)

Total height: 3.4 cm
Total length: 8.9 cm

The original reportedly excavated at
Lincheng, Shandong Province.
Historical Museum of China, Beijing.

The imperial tally, such as this example, was used to authorise imperial instructions and particularly military movements. It was carried by the messenger as his evidence of authenticity. For some reason the tiger became the adopted form for such tallies which were divided down the middle into two sections. The hollow interior may have carried an imperial seal. This example is inlaid in gold, like the original, with an inscription comprising 12 characters and which reads: **jia bing zhi fu, you zai huangdi, zuo zai yangling**: "an imperial tally for the armoured force, the right (half) with the emperor, the left (half) with Yangling."

The original cannot be opened due to the corrosion of the bronze. That the two parts were found together is probably due to the fact that they were never used.

19
Bronze Standard Weight
Total height: 7.4 cm
Weight: 250 grams
Excavated in 1976 in the vicinity of the
Qin Shihuang mausoleum, Lintong.
Shaanxi Provincial Museum, Xian.

Amongst Qin Shihuang's reorganisations of the structure of government was the standardisation of weights and measures. This bronze standard weight is tangible evidence of those reforms. It is in the shape of a bronze bell, hollow, and with a small handle. The measure has two lengthy incised inscriptions which form the complete text of the decrees issued by Qin Shihuang and his successor, the Second Emperor Qin Ershi, relating to the standardisation of measures. The First Emperor's decree reads: **erhliu nian, huangdi jin bing jian tianxia, zhu hou qianshou da an, li hao wei huangdi, nai zhao chengxiang zhuang wan, fadu liang, ze bu yi, qianyi zhe, jie ming yizhi:** "In the 26th year (221 BC) the Emperor conquered the empire, the feudal lords acknowledged his authority and there was peace. He proclaimed himself the emperor and summoned the Prime Minister Zhuang to standardise measurements. Whatever was not standard or in doubt was standardised". The Second Emperor's decree reads: **yuan nian zhi, zhao chengxiang si, qu ji, fadu liang, jinshi huangdi weizhi, jie you ke ci−. Jin xi hao, er ke ci bu chengshi huangdi, qi yujiu yuan ou, ru hou si wei zhi zhe, bu cheng cheng gong chengde. Ke ci zhao, gu ke zuo, shi wu yi:** "In the first year of his reign, (the emperor) summoned Prime Minister Li Si to eliminate abnormality and proclaim standardisation. These were the instructions of the First Emperor and had all been documented. Nowadays, in writing, people no longer follow the standardisation of the First Emperor. This deterioration is caused by the passage of time. If in the future this trend continues the great achievement (of the First Emperor) will not be followed. Therefore this decree is issued and engraved on the left (of the original decree) to dispel any doubt."

20
Bronze Standard Measure
(Reproduction)
Total length: 30.3 cm
Height: 9.8 cm
Historical Museum of China, Beijing.

A bowl-shaped oval measure with a protruding groove in which a handle could be fitted. The vessel gives the standard volume of one **dou** which on the basis of the capacity volume of this vessel is equal to 2050 millilitres.

On one side of the outside surface is engraved the First Emperor's decree of 221 BC and on the other side the Second Emperor's decree of 209 BC, both of which relate to the standardisation of weights and measures (see catalogue number 19).

21
Pottery Water Pipe
Length: 72 cm
Height: 47 cm

Excavated at the Qin Shihuang
mausoleum site, Lintong.
Shaanxi Museum of Qin Dynasty
Terracotta Warriors and Horses, Lintong.

A five-sided buff pottery moulded water pipe with a string-like pattern on the exterior surface. Such pipes were evidently made in some quantities and formed part of the drainage system for the burial pits. Water pipes of this kind were also used in other constructions, including the burial mausoleum buildings and the Qin palace at Xianyang.

22
Rectangular Pottery Brick

Length: 42 cm
Width: 18.2 cm
Depth: 9.2 cm
Weight: 13.5 g

Excavated in 1977 from Pit Number 1.
Shaanxi Museum of Qin Dynasty
Terracotta Warriors and Horses, Lintong.

A solid grey pottery brick from the floor of the number 1 burial pit. Such bricks were clearly made in very large quantities as the entire floors of all three burial pits were brick paved. This example has a fine textured body and an overall surface pattern gained from the mould.

On one edge are stamped the characters **an wei**. According to a passage in the **Lu Shi Chunqiu** (Commentary on the Spring and Autumn Annals by Lü): "Articles were stamped with the names of the craftsmen to indicate their authenticity". **An wei** may, therefore, be the name of the brickmaker.

23
Brick with Dragon Design
Length: 70 cm
Width: 39 cm
Depth: 17 cm
Excavated in 1974 from the site of the
Qin palace at Xianyang.
Xianyang City Museum, Shaanxi Province.

A hollow grey pottery brick used in the construction of the Qin imperial palace at Xianyang where it was probably part of the surrounding terrace. The brick is incised with a lively coiled dragon and other decorative motifs that would have extended on to form a continuous pattern.

24
Brick with Sun Motif

Length: 44 cm
Width: 32.5 cm
Depth: 4 cm

Excavated in 1974 from the site of the
Qin palace at Xianyang.
Xianyang City Museum, Shaanxi Province.

A thin rectangular pottery brick of greenish grey colour with an all-over decorative pattern in relief. The design is composed of parallel lines forming a lozenge pattern and with each lozenge a circular sun motif. Within the parallel line borders are decorative scroll motifs.

Pottery bricks of this kind have been discovered at both the Qin palace site at Xianyang and in the vicinity of the Qin Shihuang mausoleum. It is thought they were used for paving the floors.

25
Brick with Rhombic and Circular Pattern

Length: 34 cm
Width: 27 cm
Depth: 3 cm
Excavated in 1974 in the village of Yuchi,
north of Qin Shihuang's grave.
Shaanxi Museum of Qin Dynasty
Terracotta Warriors and Horses, Lintong.

At the centre of the tile there is a circle divided by two bowshaped lines. To the left and right are three parallel lines and a sling called a cloud pattern. Above and below the circle are four diamond shapes. There is a circle segment in each corner. The back of the tile shows a complex string pattern.

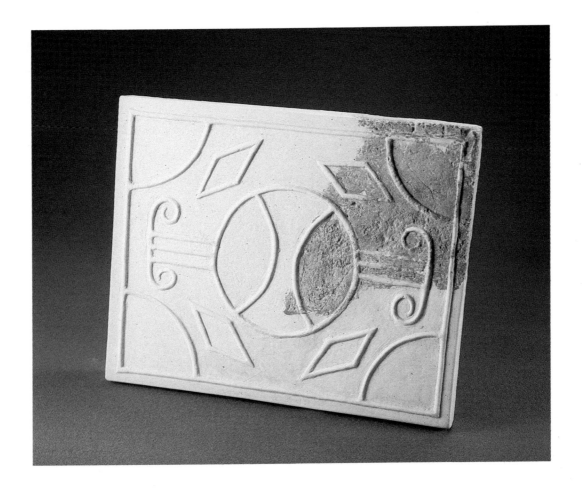

26
Brick with Lozenge Pattern
Length: 42.5 cm
Width: 31.3 cm
Depth: 4 cm
Excavated in 1976 in the village of Yuchi,
north of Qin Shihuang's grave.
Shaanxi Museum of Qin Dynasty
Terracotta Warriors and Horses, Lintong.

The decoration consists of parallel lines that form a lozenge pattern. In each square there is a circular ornament (a "**bi**" ring) with a cloud pattern. Within the parallel lines are circles and S-shaped scrolls. The back of the tile is decorated in a chequered pattern.

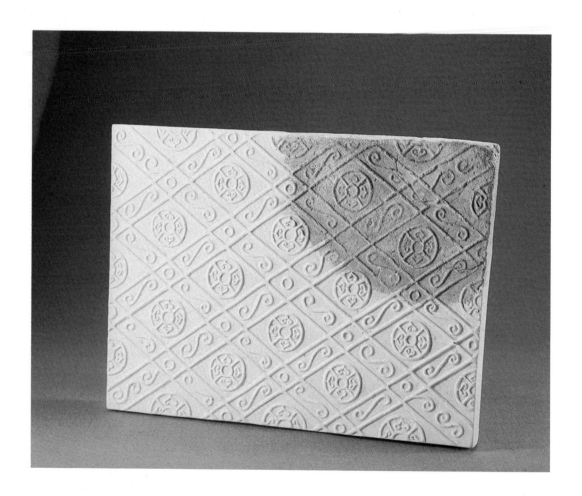

27-28

**Roof Tile Ends
with Coiled Cloud Design**

Diameter: 16.5 cm

Excavated in 1981 from the site of
Chengou, north-west of Qin Shihuang's
grave.
Shaanxi Museum of Qin Dynasty
Terracotta Warriors and Horses, Lintong.

Two typical examples of round end tiles made of terracotta. Both tiles are decorated in similar geometric pattern. A circle in the middle is surrounded by decorative scrolls usually known as a cloud design.

Roof tiles of this type were in common use at the time and have been found close to Qin Shihuang's grave and by the Qin palace in Xianyang.

29
Two Roof Tile Ends
Diameter: 16 cm (A); 16.5 cm (B)
Excavated in 1976 at the Qin Shihuang
mausoleum site, Lintong.
Shaanxi Museum of Qin Dynasty
Terracotta Warriors and Horses, Lintong.

A pair of typical circular roof tile ends possibly from one of the ancillary buildings at the Qin Shihuang burial site. Both are made of a grey pottery with moulded geometric design of similar but not identical composition.

30
Grey Pottery Jar
Height: 21.5 cm
Diameter at the mouth: 18 cm
Excavated in 1976 in the village of Yuchi,
north of Qin Shihuang's grave.
Shaanxi Museum of Qin Dynasty
Terracotta Warriors and Horses, Lintong.

   A round vessel with short neck and marked shoulders. It is decorated with circular grooves. The character **"ge"** is inscribed twice between neck and shoulder.

   The pot is made on a potter's wheel and is fired hard, and such pots were probably mass produced during this period. Many kilns from the Qin era have been found at Xianyang, varying in shape, from round to horseshoe. They are relatively small; 1 metre long and 2.2 metres wide. The same type of kiln was used for the production of bricks. It is thought the potteries were mainly a domestic industry as many terracotta objects have been found bearing inscriptions showing they were made privately as well as for the government.

31
Iron Axe
Height: 16.7 cm
Width: 11.6 cm
Excavated in 1982 from the Horse Pit
in Shangjiao Village east of Qin Shihuang's
grave.
Shaanxi Museum of Qin Dynasty
Terracotta Warriors and Horses, Lintong.

This axe belonged to one of the terracotta stableboys (cat. no. 10) and was buried together with a shortnecked pot and a lantern in one of the horse pits.

Three different types of cast iron axes were found in the pit. They were not meant to have handles and are flat. Iron was used in the manufacture of agricultural tools before being utilised for weapons. Consequently by the end of the Warring States period and during the Qin Dynasty nearly all bronze axes had been replaced by iron ones.

32
Iron Spade or Hatchet
Height: 7.5 cm
Width: 14 cm

Excavated in 1981 from the site of
Chengou, north-west of Qin Shihuang's grave
Shaanxi Museum of Qin Dynasty
Terracotta Warriors and Horses, Lintong.

33
Iron Axe
Height: 6.24 cm
Width: 5.72 cm

Excavated in 1981 from the site of
Chengou, north-west of Qin Shihuang's grave
Shaanxi Museum of Qin Dynasty
Terracotta Warriors and Horses, Lintong.

This is the blade for a small axe used for woodwork. In this exhibit the blade
is of even thickness although as a rule the blade was narrower at one end.

Chronological Table

XIA DYNASTY	c2100–1600BC		WESTERN JIN DYNASTY	265–316
SHANG DYNASTY	c1600–1027 BC		EASTERN JIN DYNASTY	317–420
WESTERN ZHOU			NORTHERN AND	
DYNASTY	1027–771 BC		SOUTHERN DYNASTIES	420–581
EASTERN ZHOU			SUI DYNASTY	581–618
DYNASTY	771–221 BC		TANG DYNASTY	618–906
Spring and			FIVE DYNASTIES	906–960
Autumn Annals	771–475 BC		SONG DYNASTY	960–1279
Warring States	475–221 BC		YUAN DYNASTY	1279–1368
QIN DYNASTY	221–206 BC		MING DYNASTY	1368–1644
WESTERN HAN			QING DYNASTY	1644–1911
DYNASTY	206 BC–8 AD		REPUBLIC OF CHINA	1911–1949
EASTERN HAN			PEOPLE'S REPUBLIC OF	
DYNASTY	25 AD–220		CHINA FOUNDED	1949
THREE KINGDOMS	220–280			

Map of China

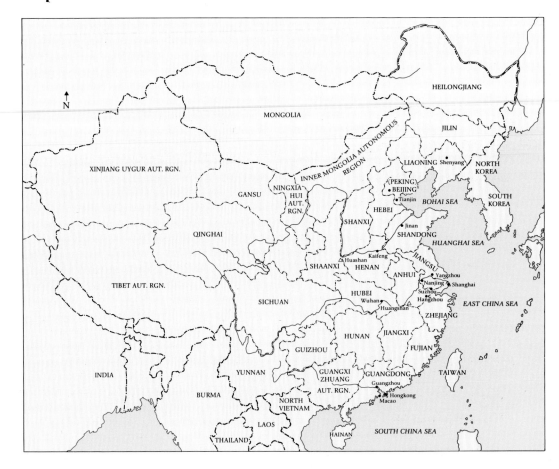

Select Bibliography

History

Bodde, Derk; **China's First Unifier. A study of the Ch'in (Qin) Dynasty as seen in the life of Li Ssu**, Leiden, 1938. Reprinted, Hong Kong, 1967.

Chavannes, Edouard; **Les Mémoires Historiques de Sse-ma Ts'ien.** 5 vols., Paris, 1895-1905.

Fitzgerald, C. P.; **China: A Short Cultural History**, first published 1935, 4th revised ed. London 1976.

Latourette, K. S.; **The Chinese: Their History and Culture**, New York, 1964.

Reischauer, E. O. and Fairbank, J. K.; **East Asia: The Great Tradition** Boston, 1970.

Watson, Burton; **Records of the Historian.** Chapters from the Shih Chi of Ssu-ma Chien (Sima Qian). New York (Columbia University Press) 1958. Reprinted 1961, 1962, 1969.

Yang, Hsien-yi and Gladys; **Selection from Records of the Historian.** Written by Szuma Chien (Sima Qian). Peking, 1979.

Philosophy

de Bary, W. D. (ed); **Sources of the Chinese Tradition**, first published 1960, 8th ed. in 2 vols., New York, 1971.

Duyvendak, J. J. L.; **The Book of Lord Shang. A Classic of the Law.** London 1928. Reprinted 1963.

Fung Yu-lan; **The Spirit of Chinese Philosophy**, London 1947. Reprinted 1962.

Fung Yu-lan; **A Short History of Chinese Philosophy** (ed. D. Bodde), New York 1960.

Hsiao Kung-chuan; **A History of Chinese Political Thought.** Vol. 1: From the Beginnings to The Sixth Century AD. Trans. by F. W. Mote, Princeton University, 1979.

Waley, Arthur; **Three Ways of Thoughts in Ancient China**, London 1946.

Watson, Burton; **Hsun Tzu: basic writings**, New York and London (Columbia University Press) 1963.

Watson, Burton; **Han Fei Tzu: basic writings**, New York and London (Columbia University Press) 1964.

Wright, A. F. (ed.); **The Confucian Persuasion**, Stanford 1960.

Art and Archaeology

Australian Art Exhibitions Corporation; **The Chinese Exhibition.** Catalogue of an Exhibition of Recent Archaeological Finds of the People's Republic of China, Melbourne 1977.

Capon, Edmund; **Art and Archaeology in China**, Melbourne 1977, MIT Boston 1977 and 1980.

Chang, Kwang-chih; **The Archaeology of Ancient China.** 3rd. ed. revised, New Haven (Yale University Press) 1977.

Cotterell, Arthur; **The First Emperor of China**, New York 1981.

Dien, Albert E. (translated) "First Report on the Exploratory Excavations of the Ch'in Pit of Pottery Figures at Lin-t'ung hsien", **Chinese Sociology and Anthropology** 10, no. 2 (Winter, 1977/78), pp. 3-50. A complete translation of the excavation report in **Wen Wu** 1975/11, pp. 1-18.

Dien, Albert E. (translated) "Excavation of the Ch'in Dynasty Pit Containing Pottery Figures of Warriors and Horses at Lin-t'ung, Shensi Province" **Chinese Studies in Archaeology** 1, no. 1 (Summer, 1979), pp. 8-55. A complete translation of the excavation report of Pit no. 2 in **Wen Wu** 1978/5, pp. 1-19.

Hearn, Maxwell; "An ancient Chinese army risen from underground sentinel duty", **Smithsonian**, November 1979.

Qian Hao, Chen Heyi and Ru Suichu **Out of China's Earth**, New York and Beijing 1981.

Rawson, Jessica; **Ancient China: Art and Archaeology**, London (British Museum) 1980.

Wen Fong (ed.); **The Great Bronze Age of China**, New York, Metropolitan Museum of Art, 1980.

Watson, William **The Genius of China.** An Exhibition of Archaeological Finds of the People's Republic of China, London 1973.

Watson, William; **China Before the Han Dynasty**, London 1961.

Watson, William; **Early Civilization in China**, London 1966.

The principal excavation reports on the Qin Shihuang burial pits have appeared in the following Chinese journals:

Wen Wu	1975	number 11
Wen Wu	1976	number 11
Wen Wu	1978	number 5
Wen Wu	1979	number 12
Kaogu	1975	number 6

Acknowledgements

Exhibitions of the importance of "The Emperor's Warriors" generally take several years to arrange. On this occasion the negotiations were completed in less than twelve months and provide a shining example of international co-operation and goodwill.

First and foremost we owe an immense debt of gratitude to the Government of the People's Republic of China for permitting such major national treasures to be displayed in Edinburgh. This generous gesture has given us the opportunity to see, at first hand, terracotta figures and other antiquities from the burial compound of the first Emperor of China, a rare privilege that is normally only open to those who are able to travel to China to visit Qin Shihuang's vast mausoleum *in situ.*

Of course, events of this nature cost a great deal to mount and publicise. In this connection, I wish to express the District Council's warm thanks for assistance received from Mirror Group Newspapers and Scottish Daily Record and Sunday Mail, Visiting Arts, the Scottish Arts Council, the British Council, Scotsman Publications, the LAS Group, British Rail and the Museums and Galleries Commission.

Numerous individuals and organisations have contributed to this enterprise. Mr Frank Dunlop, Director of the Edinburgh International Festival Society, deserves praise for drawing the exhibition to our attention in the first place and for commencing the negotiations to secure it for Edinburgh. The staff of the British Embassy in Beijing, in particular Mr Tim Butchard, have been unflagging in their support, as also have been officials of the Foreign and Commonwealth Office in London. British Council representatives in countries as far flung as Austria and Australia have expended great energy on our behalf. Much useful practical advice has been freely given by Dr Jan Wirgin of Stockholm, Professor Hans Mayr and Frau Temel of Vienna and Dr Lu Shaochen of China. Also, it gives me great pleasure to record that Edinburgh's Chinese Community have afforded us considerable help.

Finally, this project has benefited from the enthusiastic support of Mr Bernard Connolly, Director of Recreation and many other District Council colleagues. But above all, Ms Shiona Airlie's indefatigable curatorial work, Mr Alexander Topp's design flair and Mr David Williams' prodigious marketing efforts merit special commendation.

Herbert Coutts
City Curator

Published by the City of Edinburgh Museums and Art Galleries, Department of Recreation, City of Edinburgh District Council.

Improving Services—Creating Jobs

Designed and produced by Graphic Partners, Edinburgh
Printed by Waddie & Co. Ltd., Edinburgh and London